nder the age of seaven and fifty years. They shall be of the
oorest and needyest people first of the parish of Lee who have
ved orderly and supported themselves by their honest labour
n the younger dayes and if there be not enough such found
n the parish of Leigh then of the said parish of Lewisham
nd if not there then of the said parish of Greenwich. Upon
very vacancy the said Master and Wardens shall in the first
lace give notice thereof to the Minister Churchwardens or
verseers for the poor of the said parish of Lee to present unto
hem some fit person soe qualified as aforesaid toe supply that
acancy and if they shall not present one within two weeks
fter such notice then they shall give like notice to the Minister
hurchwardens or overseers of the said parish of Lewisham
nd in default of their presenting a fit person within two weeks
fter such notice the said Master and Wardens shall give notice
o the Minister Churchwardens or overseers of the parish of
Greenwich that parish which shall present any poor old man
r woman to have the benefit of the said almeshouses shall by
wo or more of their substantial parishioners give Bond unto
he said Master and Wardens in the penalty of twenty pounds
0 susleyne [?] and relieve the person presented in the time of
is or her sicknesse or other healthlesse condition when their
veekly and annuall allowance within mentioned may not be
ufficient to support them and alsoe to see them decently and
hristianly buryed at their charge towards which charge such
parish shall have all the goods and chattels which shall belong
o the deceased person by them presented shall afterwards
ppeare to the said Master and Wardens to have been an
nfit person to be admitted into the said almes houses at his
r their admission or shall deserve in the judgement of the
aid Master and Wardens to be removed and expulsed out of
he said almeshouses that then such person upon two months
varning to be given by the said Master and Wardens or any of
hem or any person appointed by them shall avoid out of and
rom the said almes houses and peaceably yield and deliver up
he possession thereof unto the said Master and Wardens or to
uch as they shall appoint and that the parish shall provide
or them - The said almes people shall be such as can say
y heart the Lords prayer the Apostles Creed and the Tenn
Commandments or shall be bound to learne soe to doe within
wo months after their admission in the said almeshouses or
lse they shall be expelled thence. The said almespeople shall
very Lords day come to the Parish Church of Lee to hear
ivine Service and the word of God preached forenoone and
fternoone and alsoe to the prayers in the Chappell Mundays
nd Saturdays at the hours appointed and for every default
hall forfeit four pence to the said Schoole Mistresse who is to
ave an eye upon them herein unless in the case of sickness
r other good cause to be allowed of by the said Masters and
Vardens The wilful and obstinate neglectors of Divine Service

either in the said Parish Church — — — — — — shall
be finally expulsed out — — — — — — — — mes
people shall not entert — — — — — — — — uild
or other inmate to lo — — — — — — — out
of their houses above — — — — — — out
good cause to be allow — — — — — — ens
upon paine of expulsio — — — — — ne
sweet and wholesome — — — — — lls boards
timber glasse windows and all that belongs to their respective
apartments. They shall suffer no dirt filth foule water or other
noysomenesse to be thrown into the water ditch or streame on
the north side of the said almes houses the offenders therein
shall incur such forfeiture as the said Master and Wardens
shall in their discretion think fit and in case of wilful persisting
in such offence shall be expelled. They shall not throw out dirt
ashes or other filth in the street nor keep any such noisome
or offensive things within their particular apartments or
within the places there to enjoy in comon there being provided
a convenient place for that purpose just without the wall at
the west end of the said almshouses with a door opening out
thereunto. They shall keep their houses of offices clean and
sweet without throwing any dirt filth or rubbish thereinto this
to be done by weekly termes. That for the men by the man
each his week and that for the women by the woman each
her week and they shall give timely notice to the said Master
and Wardens for having the said houses of offices emptied as
need shall require. They shall keep under the wall on the south
side of the said almeshouses clean and every day swept that
no stoppage may happen therein and shall keep their grasse
platt or dying place clean and greene and their small Kitchen
Garden well planted with pott herbs and sowed from time to
time with convenient seed for that purpose and shall keep it
always neate and well weeded and shall keep their washhouse
brewhouse or bakehouse well swept clean sweet and wholesome
all which and all other publique places and accommodations
which they are to enjoy in common they shall take care of by
weekly termes both Men and Women. They shall live quietly
peaceably and in good charity one with another and behave
themselves orderly one towards another as becomes Christians
and if any of them shall quarrell scolde raile sweare of otherwise
misbehave him or herself hee or she soe offending shall forfeit
fourpence to the Schoole Mistresse for every such offence and it
the same offence shall be committed above three times then the
offender shall be expelled out of the said almeshouses. The said
almespeople shall not plant any trees against any of the walls
of the said almeshouses or Chappell. None shall be admitted
into the said almeshouses that hath any noysom or incurable
disease. Every of the said almespeople as also the said School
Mistresse shall take all special care to prevent Fire in the said
almeshouses

1: interior of the chapel, September 2007

Boone's Chapel

history in the making

Madeleine Adams and Charlie MacKeith
with Ian Mills

Contents

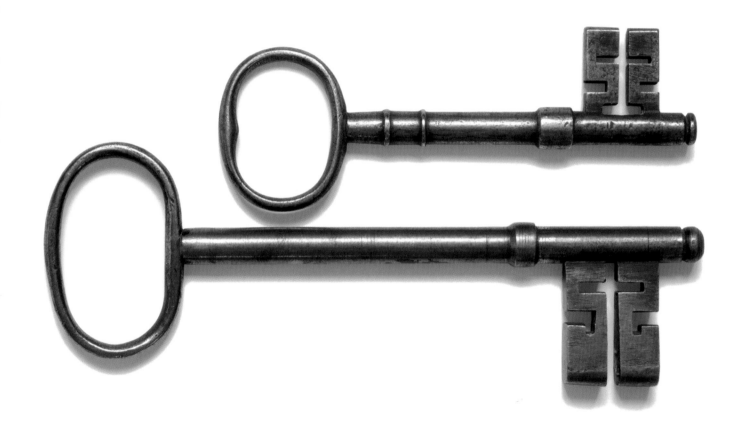

2: the chapel keys |———————| 2cm

Foreword

One of the most exciting features of the last 25 years has been the way a whole succession of interesting buildings in Blackheath – symbols of the area's history and architectural development – have re-emerged, for the most part gloriously, from the ravages of the Blitz, neglect, occasional misuse and threatened demolition.

It might seem invidious to list some of these buildings but the Paragon was an early example of this process and more recent buildings I can personally recall being rescued include, to the undying credit of the Blackheath Society, the Blackheath Preservation Trust and others, Chapman House and the Concert Halls in the Village, Eagle House (Tesco's unlikely contribution) on Lewisham Hill, Wyberton House and The Hollies on Lee Terrace, The School of Art building at the end of Bennett Park, the Conservatoire at the top of the Village and the Manor House in Old Road. They also include St Margaret, Lee, the repair of which took 18 years and cost £3.5 million, and the Boone's Chapel, one of only two Grade 1 listed buildings in the London Borough of Lewisham.

At a personal level the chapel's rescue is the story of three kindred spirits discovering each other, pursuing the fulfilment of a common vision and overcoming a series of challenges that were partly rooted in the bureaucracy of some of the funding agencies, partly created by the discovery of the mortal remains of Christopher and Mary Boone in a hidden vault and partly inherent in the technical difficulty of much of the repair and conservation work. I first met Madeleine Adams, and then Charlie MacKeith, in early September 2004. Instantly, we discovered a shared passion, romantic (even sentimental) in its roots, but also hard-edged, determined and business-like. The single objective was to repair and conserve the chapel and make it a work place which, as architects, Madeleine and Charlie could have only previously dreamt about. For them, the chapel was a case of love at first sight and the Blackheath Historic Buildings Trust, the means of fulfilling a dream. For me and my Trust, they were kindred spirits and the tenants I had been looking for but failing to find for more than a year. The prospect of rescuing the chapel and giving it a new and dynamic purpose strongly resonated with their affection for the Blackheath area and their professional and personal enthusiasm for its history and architecture.

It may seem far-fetched but the more I have looked at the chapel as it has slowly been brought back to life, the more I have been reminded of a moment in my past, back in early October 1962, when I stood captivated by the Taj Mahal. The Taj and the chapel are totally different in scale, architectural style, colour and decoration. However, both buildings are perfectly proportioned, both have unostentatious decoration, both look like caskets or jewel cases and both are places of burial, heavy in atmosphere and history.

The architect of the chapel could have been Wren but was probably Hooke. It is architecture typical of the style of the late 17th century and reflects the confidence which characterised the City of London's response to the Great Fire. Read the fascinating story of the chapel set out so well in this book. Then visit or revisit this piece of local history on one of its exhibition days. Outside, enjoy a structure which in its perfect proportions and understated decoration is as good an example of one of the best periods of architectural history as you will find in south east London, Greenwich notwithstanding. Inside, enjoy the stucco embellishment, the fine timber panelling and the floor of Purbeck stone hewn from the same Dorset quarry used by Christopher Boone in the 1680s and, if you are lucky, meet Madeleine and Charlie. Without their vision, skill and hard work, the chapel would probably not have survived.

Ian Mills, Chair, Blackheath Historic Buildings Trust
July 2010

3: the front door, June 2005

Introduction

Boone's Chapel, on the A20 in Lewisham, was built by Christopher and Mary Boone in 1682 with four almshouses at the entrance to their Lee Place estate in the village of Lee. At that time Lee was in rural Kent, six miles southeast of the City of London. The chapel stands in the grounds of Regency almshouses, glimpsed over the boundary wall along the A20, in stark contrast to the surrounding bustle of a 21st century London Red Route. Since moving to the area in 1996 the abandoned building captivated us. It appeared from occasional press reports that refurbishment was in hand. Shortly after establishing our practice in Blackheath a 'to let' board appeared on the chapel in August 2004 (fig 4). This was our first introduction to Ian Mills, the Blackheath Historic Buildings Trust and two earlier attempts to restore the building spearheaded by local historian Neil Rhind. It was also the beginning of our immersion in the history of the chapel and immediate area.

The Blackheath Historic Buildings Trust (BHBT) was established as a charity in 1999 by the Blackheath Preservation Trust (BPT) to raise public funds for the repair and conservation of the chapel. BPT, as a company using commercial development models to save local historic buildings, could not secure this funding. There had been earlier schemes to redevelop the site to raise money for the chapel's restoration. One such scheme by Niall Phillips Architects in 1996 included three pavilions of sheltered housing (fig 5). This scheme won planning consent and funding. However, the BHBT trustees were determined to find a solution that would not block the views of the large trees and landscaped garden of the almshouses. Under Ian Mills' chairmanship, in 2003 the BHBT secured the earlier offer of funding support from the Heritage Lottery Fund (HLF) and English Heritage (EH) totalling £320,000 for a stand alone scheme, and set out to repair and conserve the chapel in partnership with a tenant for the restored building.

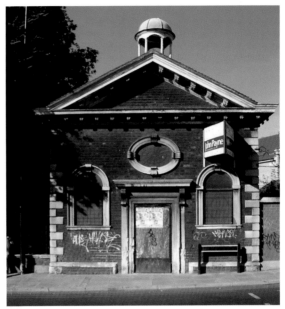

4: August 2004

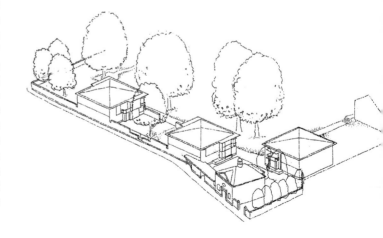

5: scheme by Niall Phillips Architects, 1996

11

Even when derelict it was obvious that the chapel would be an extraordinary studio with its rich history, beautiful light and garden. Our interest did not have a commercial logic. The building was an opportunity to test some of our ideas evolved through teaching and work for clients on similar buildings. Experience of museum and exhibition design had led us to look for a way of working that would allow direct engagement with building users and visitors. As the funding conditions required that the chapel should be open to the public 30 days a year, it looked like our business model would be tested.

The first 18 months of the project focused on legal and funding formalities. The chapel freehold was, and still is, owned by the Merchant Taylors' Company (MTC). The BHBT held a 99 year lease that would be passed to the final tenants following repairs. To secure the funding our practice proposed to pay the difference between the grants and final building costs as rent in advance. This was checked by the funders as there could be no private gain for a publicly funded project.

The building had been changed significantly in the nineteenth century and was in a poor state from 60 years of neglect. This was a once in a lifetime opportunity to see if original elements could be recreated. Our search for complete records of the building prior to major changes in the late nineteenth century proved elusive. But we were immediately drawn into a history of tantalising anecdotes, strangely rewarding dead ends and glimpses of long vanished personal lives. The following chapter on the history of the chapel is the result of research in a number of archives, guided by numerous experts in their respective fields. The assistance of Alfred Wood, Lee's pre-eminent historian, has been invaluable. Through the meticulous work of Bob Boone we have been able to correct some accepted facts with confidence. Bob, an American from a different branch of the family, has been avidly researching all family branches for over 20 years.

Understanding the history allowed us to determine how the requirements of modern uses and services could be incorporated without losing the clarity of the original building. The first decision was to distinguish between public use and everyday office use. The south doors to the street are only used by the public when the office equipment is cleared away and the full extent of the room can be seen. In private use a new hidden door on the north serves as the office entrance with access across a garden path to an annexe, a stand alone service building that contains a kitchen, toilet and boiler. Early discussions with the BHBT suggested that other tenants and different uses might follow, so the timber framed annexe was designed as part of the boundary garden wall that could be easily removed. Its separation from the chapel allows neighbouring almshouse residents access to Lee High Road as well as preserving the chapel's appearance, following changes in the nineteenth century, as a perfect casket, visible on all sides.

With every building project the process of making, either in a workshop or on site, is the final, exciting stage that gives shape to the ideas behind a design. Assisted by Rickards Conservation, other specialist consultants, suppliers and craftspeople we learned to understand what might be possible. The processes, described in chapter 4, told us other stories about the possible history and making of the original building. The building, its history and the objects uncovered are modest and, maybe, insignificant. However, the response and support of local people, and the experience of working day-to-day in such a fabulous place, revealed through Tim Crocker's photographs, have proved well worth the emotional and financial investment. Our developing use of the chapel since completion will continue to consume as much energy as its rescue, but it will be worth it.

Madeleine Adams and Charlie MacKeith
Research Design and Boone's Chapel, 2010

6: west door, September 2007

7: interior seen through the west door,
September 2007

8: interior, west door,
September 2007

9: south west window, September 2007

10: north window with discovered artefacts
and the 1826 almshouses beyond,
September 2007

11: north elevation, September 2007

12: the 1826 almshouse garden,
September 2007

3   History

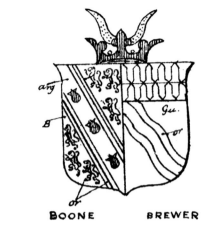

BOONE   BREWER

13: top, the Boone and Brewer coat of arms
14: bottom, Lee Place

The Boones and Lee Place

Apart from a few short references in contemporary documents, the chapel, the surviving charity, a family mausoleum and a street name are the only evidence of the Lee branch of the Boone family. Christopher Boone, and his wife Mary, appear to have slipped through the comprehensive net of Restoration tales and histories of influential people. The following summary is based on legal records, a few letters and diary entries. Anecdotal evidence hints at the couple's connections to the highest level of the business and cultural life of the City. A more detailed study than this will be needed when firmer evidence, maybe even a portrait, is found.

Christopher was born in 1616 in Taunton, Somerset, to Christopher Boone, a wool merchant, and Anne Dryver (née Pysing), a rich widow from Hay, Somerset. He joined the family trade making his fortune trading in Spanish and west country wools. Letters from John Paige in 1654 describe Boone's trade in Spanish wines. He was one of 24 commissioners of the East India Company (EIC) confirmed by Charles II on his accession and featured regularly in EIC treasury matters. Samuel Pepys refers in his diary to an incident when Boone and three other EIC directors were called '*on their knees*' to the House of Lords over a libel dispute in 1668. He was a member of the Merchant Taylors' Company (MTC) and was admitted to the freedom of the City of London yet, for someone so influential in commercial affairs, he received no public office or civil honour. The reason might lie in family connections with Cromwell and the Protectorate.

A relation, Thomas Boone, MP for Dartmouth, was appointed as a judge at Charles I's trial by Parliament, although he declined to attend. Christopher's life appears to be similar to that of many City merchants who made their fortunes under Cromwell yet were accepted by Charles II, because the king needed their money through taxes, loans or the purchase of Crown property.

One such parcel of land in Hereford was acquired by Christopher and was central to his endowment of the chapel and charity. Christopher is recorded in the parish register as being buried on 22 July 1686 '*in linen*'. That his wife was able to pay for him to be buried in linen, rather than in wool as prescribed by law, would appear to have been more important to the writers of the register than his charitable acts. His will reveals other details of his character and past: equal amounts of money were left to the reading of the Gospel in New England and to many other almshouses and poor charities in London and his birthplace.

Mary Boone, née Brewer, was born in Bishopsgate in 1634, to John Brewer, a grocer living in St Bartholomew Exchange, and Dorothy, widow of John Bowater. Her marriage to Christopher brought a dowry of £10,000. After Christopher's death, a wedding licence of 1688 between Mary and the Right Hon. John, Earl of Oxenstern was filed in Greenwich. The marriage would appear not to have been finalised. Her signature (fig 15) appears on an indenture of 1707 that includes the rental of Pentlands, another large house in Lee purchased by the couple. Mary is recorded in the parish register as being buried in '*her chapel... in a coffin lined with velvet*' in 1722.

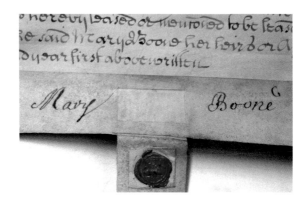

15: Mary Boone's signature 1707

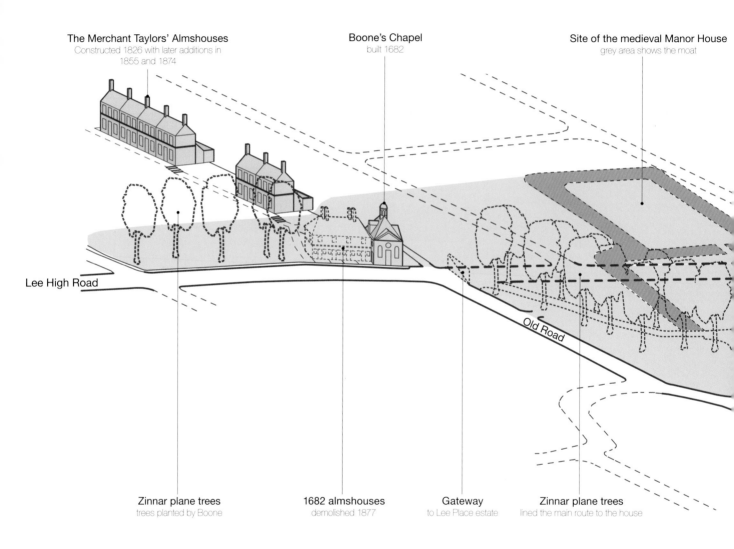

The Merchant Taylors' Almshouses
Constructed 1826 with later additions in
1855 and 1874

Boone's Chapel
built 1682

Site of the medieval Manor House
grey area shows the moat

Lee High Road

Old Road

Zinnar plane trees
trees planted by Boone

1682 almshouses
demolished 1877

Gateway
to Lee Place estate

Zinnar plane trees
lined the main route to the house

16: diagram looking north showing historic changes to part of the village of Lee

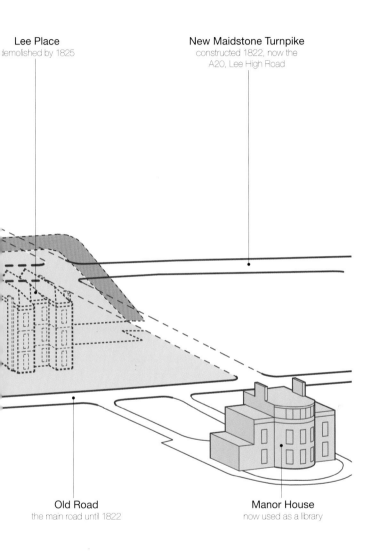

Lee Place
demolished by 1825

New Maidstone Turnpike
constructed 1822, now the
A20, Lee High Road

Old Road
the main road until 1822

Manor House
now used as a library

Christopher and Mary moved to Lee some time after 1668. Their house, Lee Place, stood on the site of the present day Market Parade on the A20. According to local historian Josephine Birchenough, Lee Place was built in 1662 to replace the medieval manor house of Lee, located on the site of today's Lee Church Street Primary School. The medieval moat of the manor house was retained as a garden feature following Boone's purchase of the house in 1668 from Col. George Thomson, a member of Cromwell's Council of State, and was still present at the sale and breaking up of the estate in 1824 (figs 28 and 29).

The house was the largest in Lee with 21 chimneys recorded in a chimney tax before Boone's purchase. Plans of the house are in the Rawlinson Collection in the Bodleian Library, Oxford. The manor house title, having lapsed, was later taken by the Barings for their house, now a local library and park, on the Old Road. Figure 16 shows the house and grounds in diagrammatic form looking north in the context of today's roads, in stark contrast to the landscape of fields shown in the first MTC plan of the site in 1800 (fig 17).

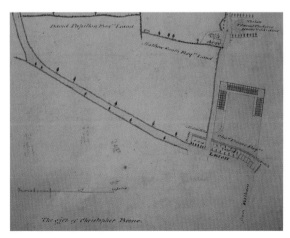

17: plan, 1800, updated in 1840 with
the 1826 MTC almshouses in red

The most personal glimpses of the couple's life in Lee are to be found in John Evelyn's diary and in the 1683 legal documentation for their charity. The motivation for the latter may simply have been a Christian interest in the care of the poor and a lasting act by a childless couple. Similar to many rich philanthropists in the Restoration, the Boones constructed and funded a chapel and almshouses, a home for poor older people. The inspiration may have been set by local examples (such as the Abraham Colfe almshouses of 1662 originally located on Lewisham High Street), by other examples in London or even by examples in the Spanish Low Countries. Like many similar private charities, to ensure its long term future, it was placed in trust with an established charitable organisation, in this case the MTC. The future financial stability of the charity had to be assured and the legal documents for Christopher Boone's charity itemise revenues in great detail. The schedule that defines the criteria for the occupants, is reproduced on the front fly leaf and page 1. The indenture, the legal summary is reproduced from page 111 onwards. Amidst the legal terminology are local descriptions (Berryhill, the brickfield, the Dungplace…) and preoccupations with everything from planting to religious duties, from sewing to cleanliness.

John Evelyn's 3 visits to the house add even more detail. The garden is celebrated by noting Christopher's importation of 'Zinnar' plane trees, which survive in the grounds today (fig 18), to protect against the plague. The cultural aspirations of the pair, especially Mary, are described through their commissioning of the leading Dutch sculptor, Grinling Gibbons, discovered and promoted by Evelyn. It may be too fanciful a link but HS Glenister, in his book on great craftsmen, proposes that Gibbons' fame was a result of his work at Lee Place.

The Memoirs of John Evelyn Vol. 3
Edited by William Bray, London 1827

31 August 1679
After evening service to see a neighbour, one Mr Bohun, related to my Sonn's late tutor of that name, a rich Spanish merchant, living in a neate place, which he has adorned with many curiosities, especialy severall carvings of Mr Gibbons, and some pictures by Streeter.

30 July 1682
Went to visit our good neighbour Mr Bohun, whose house is a cabinet of all elegancies, especially Indian; in the hall are contrivances of Japan skreens instead of wainscot; and there is an excellent pendule clock inclos'd in the curious flower-work of Mr Gibbons in the middle of the vestibule. The landskips of the skreens represent the manner of living, and country of the Chinese. But above all, his lady's cabinet is adorn'd on the fret, ceiling and chimney piece, with Mr Gibbons' best carving. There are also some of Streeter's best paintings, and many rich curiosities in gold and silver as growing in the mines. The gardens are exactly kept, and the whole place very agreeable and well water'd. The owners are good neighbours and Mr Bohun has also built and endow's an hospital for eight poor people, with a pretty chapell, and every necessarie accommodation.

16 September 1683
At the elegant villa and garden of Mr Bohun's at Lee. He showed me the zinnar tree or platanus, and told me that since they had planted this kind of tree about the citty of Isaphan in Persia, the plague, which formerly much infested the place, had exceedingly abated of its mortal effects and rendered it very healthy.

18: a leaf from one of the surviving *Zinnar* plane trees

19: the original Christopher Boone's almshouses attached to the chapel prior to 1876; see figure 39 for details of the carved crest above the second almshouse door from the left

The chapel and almshouses

The 1683 Indenture provides a pragmatic description of dimensions, purpose, rules, costs, disposal of waste and a place for burials. Possibly because of Evelyn's reference to Gibbons, nineteenth century local historians proposed the highest contemporary architectural pedigree for the chapel. Sir Christopher Wren is often cited as the architect, although this was discounted when a definitive list of Wren's projects was established between 1924 and 1943. Morden College in Blackheath was the only local building, south of the Heath, to be credited to Wren in this review, although even this is now thought to be the work of a master mason, Edward Strong. Wren, as Surveyor of the King's Works, might reasonably have taken a commission from a fellow member of the MTC then passed it down a sub-contract chain of draughtsmen and builders who carried out much of his work. Alternatively, the building might have been contracted directly to a local master builder using pattern books (handbooks for builders of standard construction details and classical details) and local examples for reference.

Despite the investment in the construction and establishment of the charity, the earliest surviving drawn record of the site is the 1800 small scale plan (fig 17). The chapel and almshouses stood on the King's Highway to Maidstone and the Kent coast, an important route for communication with shipping, and the supply of the City. The chapel marked the entrance to Lee Place at a sharp bend in the highway, on what is today Old Road, as it meandered through rural Kent. The four houses attached to the chapel were simple, traditional brick structures with a steep pitched tiled roof with tall chimneys and a Dutch gabled garden wall (fig 19). The plans of the houses reflect the MTC plans of its Rosemary Lane almshouses and those of other livery companies with one room per floor off a door to the street. The overall asymmetrical composition of houses and chapel is peculiar but the details of the chapel are highly resolved.

The chapel is a single storey room, rectangular in plan with a short projection for the altar to the north, rather than the east as is normal for churches. It is constructed in brick with Portland stone rusticated quoins (blocks at each corner), door surrounds (to south and west) and window architraves. The hipped, tiled roof is capped by a timber and lead cupola that once held a bell. As first built there were just two pediments, to the south and east, probably originally covered in lead or copper. The roof cornices and pediments have white painted timber *modillions* (brackets). Decorative details, such as the stone scrolls to windows and south door, are used sparingly. Daniel Lysons, in his record of the '*Environs of London*' of 1796, describes the interior of the chapel as having the Boones' coat of arms (fig 13) above '*a vault for the Founders' family*'. The interior might also have been embellished with the Lord's Prayer, the Commandments and the Royal coat of arms as at Morden College, Blackheath, completed in 1707. The detailing of panelling in Boone's Chapel (fig 8) suggests that box pews might have been provided as at Morden College.

20: interior of Morden College Chapel

The ceiling is flat and plain with a deep coved cornice and the heads and wings of angels at each corner. The altar recess has an ornate plaster relief of flowers and angels in a curved arch springing from the high oak panelling that wraps around the room. The line of the panelling is broken only by the doors and south and north windows (figs 1 and 8). The floor was a distinctive '*Mitchell*' or diamond pattern of Purbeck tiles 45cm (18") square. No evidence has been found of the original altar floor treatment. The chapel was constructed with pews, an altar and pulpit (or reading desk) but all fittings were removed over time. Restored to its original colour scheme, the plainness of the room masks the expense and subtlety of the detailing.

The building was recorded by various trainee architects in the twentieth century. John Broome and John Stammers in 1935 completed measured drawings of the chapel, now held by the Royal Institute of British Architects Drawings Collection. In 1929 Roderick Cowley, for an essay on the almshouses of southeast London, measured the MTC almshouses and photographed the chapel, giving us the earliest record of the interior (fig 38). The building up of the road over time to the level of the south door threshold has altered the original proportions of the design. The main entrance was probably approached by steps.

There are simple geometrical proportions underlying the plan, elevations and even the south oval window. These could simply be the result of good drawing practice of which a master builder would be more than capable. However, the precise classical detailing of the modillions is based on examples in architectural books that were not widely available until the early eighteenth century (fig 22). The roof timbers of the chapel are oak, supported on two simple trusses either side of the internal cupola structure. The Baroque detailing of the windows, with Ionic volutes or scrolls at the cardinal points is also a distinctive detail.

A local building completed in 1672, the Gazebo in the grounds of the Grange, Crooms Hill, Greenwich (fig 21), has very similar timber details to those of the chapel. Beryl Platts, a local historian attributed the Gazebo to Robert Hooke, the mastermind of the Royal Society's operations and experiments as well as Wren's principal sub-contractor for architectural designs. It was built for William Turner, son in law of Sir William Hooker and associate of Boone. Again the potential connections are circumstantial, but Hooker was a leading member of the MTC and appointed Robert Hooke for changes to the MTC hall in Threadneedle Street. Drs Saunders and Davies in their 2004 history of the MTC suggest that the Boone's almshouses and chapel may have been the work of Hooke. His diary records the preparation of plans for a '*hospitall*' (an almshouse) in 1679 but the designer of the chapel may never be known. Our search was simply to try to find accurate information on the interior before changes in the nineteenth century.

21: the Gazebo, the Grange, Greenwich c1672

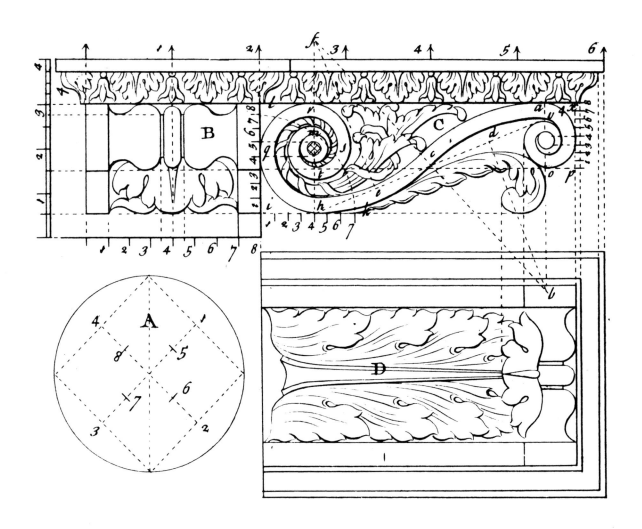

22: a Corinthian modillion from B+T Langley's 'The Builder's Jewel' 1741

The chapel and the parish

Almshouse residents were drawn from the area and were integrated into the workings of the village. Parish records indicate that almshouse residents earned money from taking in washing and laying out the dead. From the outset, the chapel functioned as a private place of worship for the founders and residents with services held by the clergy of the local parish church, St Margaret, Lee. The church, in part dating back to 1085 (fig 24), was then situated in its small graveyard opposite the north end of Brandram Road. All the almshouse residents and the twelve children were required to attend the chapel on Mondays and Saturdays to recite the Catechism, the Lord's Prayer, the Apostles Creed and the Ten Commandments. Attendance was also required at the parish church on Sundays. A key test for residents was the ability to recite the Lord's Prayer from memory.

The Reverend John Jackson, Rector of St Margaret's between 1672 and 1701, was the first chaplain and he and his successors were responsible for instructing a member of the St Margaret's clergy to ensure that the almshouse clerk swept out the chapel and rang the bell in the cupola before services and read prayers twice a week. Their annual stipend for this was £10 but for every failure to fulfil the weekly commitment, they forfeited two shillings.

Despite the founders' requirement that the chapel would be consecrated, the records of the three dioceses and the archdiocese of Canterbury, all responsible for the area at various times, suggest that it never was. However, on several occasions it doubled up as the parish church when St Margaret's was altered. The first time was 1812-1813 when the old medieval church was being enlarged and embellished by Joseph Gwilt (fig 26).

There were also three other occasions when works were being undertaken in the nave of the present Victorian church of St Margaret's: in 1870 during major repairs and redecoration, in 1873 when John Brown's galleries were being dismantled and in 1888 when James Brook's pine vault was being suspended below Brown's original lath and plaster ceiling. During the first of these periods a horse and cart driven from Eltham to London down the Old Road failed to negotiate the sharp corner to the south of the chapel and crashed into the doors to the consternation of worshippers.

23: the Boone family vault in St Margaret's churchyard, Lee constructed in 1749

24: left, the church of St Margaret, Lee drawn by IC Barrow c 1790

25: top left, George Lock and top right, Frederick Henry Law, two 19th century rectors who oversaw services in the chapel and transformed the parish church

26: above, drawing of Gwilt's church of St Margaret, Lee, 1813 and demolished in 1841

The Merchant Taylors arrive

Following the resolution of Mary's will, the Merchant Taylors' Company (MTC) assumed control of the charity in 1723 as set out in the 1683 indenture. As Mary and Christopher were childless, the estate passed in turn to another Christopher, the son of Boone's cousin, Thomas. Christopher settled at Lee Place and his son, yet another Thomas, inherited it in turn. He died in 1749 and was the first Boone to be interred in a vault in the old churchyard of St Margaret, Lee (fig 23). The parish register records the burial of his infant daughter Sarah in the chapel in 1733. Thomas left instructions that his surviving natural child, Mary Cornforth was to be allowed to live at Lee Place and '*not to be interfered with by any of the Boone family*'.

The estate passed to Thomas' nephew Charles Boone who died in 1819. His will left instructions for his return to life 100 years after his burial. Despite a welcoming party he failed to appear. Charles' daughter, Lady Harriet Drummond inherited the estate and sold it in 1824. The sale of the estate coincided with the Maidstone turnpike being straightened to its current path, bisecting the estate. Lee Place was purchased by Matthew Smith, the then owner of Pentlands, who demolished it.

The MTC had managed their own almshouses since the 15th century at various locations which included Threadneedle Street and Tower Hill in the City of London. However, by the early 19th century these dwellings were in need of repair and land in the City was expensive and in short supply. The company purchased the whole of the estate north of the turnpike at auction (figs 28, 29). Various plans by the company's surveyor, William Jupp Jr, were prepared and the final selected version was completed in 1826 (fig 30). The new company almshouses comprised 30 single bedroom cottages with paired front doors grouped in three blocks around a formal open quadrangle. The overall composition is simple and executed in a plain, Regency classical architecture. The elevations facing the open garden court are in pale yellow London stock bricks (greyed with age) and Portland stone surrounds and cornices. The central pediment and the gateway of the porter's lodge on Brandram Road (added in 1855) bear the distinctive MTC crest with its supportive camels and paschal lamb (the badge of the company's patron saint, St John the Baptist) (fig 27). Four more cottages were added prior to 1877 to the south east corner near the chapel.

The two charities on the site were run independently although the new residents had access to the chapel. The rector at this time, George Lock, with the completion of the new church of St Margaret's in 1841, attempted to have all chapel services moved to the new church. Accounts in the MTC surveyor's books record some minor changes to the chapel. In 1828 proposals were drawn up to install a damp proof course under the stone floor. Due to the cost, a timber floor was installed over the stone instead. In 1869 a new direct fired gas radiator was installed along with new seating.

27: MTC crest above Brandram Road entrance (1855)

Twelve Acres of Building Ground,

AT LEE, NEAR BLACKHEATH,
KENT.

Specifications

OF SUNDRY VALUABLE PARCELS OF

Freehold Building Ground

VERY DELIGHTFULLY SITUATE IN THE MOST BEAUTIFUL PART OF THE MUCH ADMIRED

VILLAGE OF LEE,

ONLY SIX MILES FROM LONDON,

COMPRISING

TWELVE ACRES,

BEING

THE ORNAMENTAL PADDOCK AND PLEASURE GROUNDS

FORMERLY ATTACHED TO

LEE PLACE MANSION,

The ancient Residence of the Boone Family.

The LAND will be divided into LOTS, varying from HALF an ACRE to an ACRE and HALF, and in one instance to THREE ACRES,

CONTAINING

A PICTURESQUE ISLAND & HANDSOME PIECE OF WATER;

AND THE WHOLE BEING

RICH PASTURE LAND,

Will afford opportunities for the Purchasers to form DETACHED VILLAS with PADDOCKS.

Which will be Sold by Auction,

BY MESSRS. DRIVER,

AT THE AUCTION MART,

On FRIDAY, the 22nd Day of OCTOBER, 1824, at 12 o'Clock,

IN TEN LOTS, WITHOUT ANY RESERVE.

Printed Specifications, with engraved Plans annexed, may be had at the GREEN MAN, Blackheath; LION AND LAMB, Lewisham; SHIP, Greenwich; TIGER'S HEAD, Lee Green; at the AUCTION MART; and of Messrs. DRIVER, Surveyors and Land Agents, 13, New Bridge Street, Blackfriars.

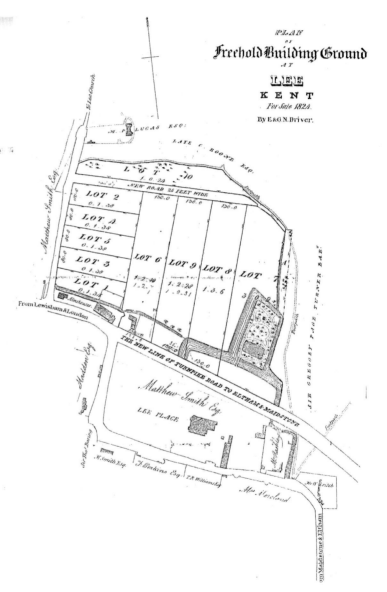

28: advertisement for the Boone estate auction 1824   29: auction lot plan 1824

30: perspective elevation in watercolours by Jupp
   of the final, constructed design 1824-5

31: section through a typical cottage in watercolours
by Roderick Cowley 1929

37

The chapel stands alone

The MTC purchase of the estate included land in addition to the almshouse site. The arrival of the railway to Blackheath in 1849 turned the estate fields into valuable building land and long leases were offered. The resulting construction on Brandram Road, Belmont Park and around Boone Street established the modern character of the area. Lee was no longer part of rural Kent as the village was being subsumed into the growing conurbation. The resulting increase in income to the charity coincided with the need to upgrade the original almshouses, by then nearly 200 year old, and to increase the number of residents. As early as 1858 plans commenced to replace Boone's almshouses and reorder the charity. A new site was purchased in 1872 half a mile east along the A20 at Lampmead Road. In 1876 the Boone's charity residents were moved to new almshouses designed by EB l'Anson with a new Victorian Boone's Chapel in the centre of the complex (fig 35).

The original 1682 almshouses were demolished in 1877 providing £84.1.6 to the MTC from the sale of materials. The only surviving fragment of the houses, a worn MTC crest (fig 39), was found in the grounds in 2005. The old chapel was retained and adapted by the MTC, with a new pedimented west wall and additional windows in this elevation, into a stand-alone building to serve all the almshouse residents of the area as a reading room and library (figs 33, 37, 38).

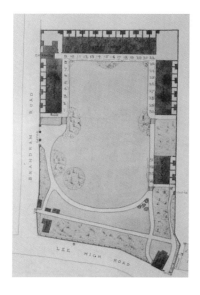

32: top, plan of current arrangement of chapel and MTC almshouses c1882
33: bottom, photograph of the chapel after demolition of the houses c1900

The chapel fulfilled its role as a reading room until 1940 but with the advent of the Blitz the building became a store for furniture salvaged from nearby houses destroyed or damaged in air raids. In 1942 the ornate wrought iron railings above the wall bordering the A20 to the south of the gardens were removed as part of the war effort apart from a 5 metre strip retained to the west of the chapel which is still in place today. Early in the war air-raid shelters were constructed north of the chapel under the large central lawn.

With the war won, on 8 May 1945 the chapel was used for a special thanksgiving service to celebrate Victory in Europe (VE) Day. After this it was boarded up and left without a role and this remained the position with its fabric slowly deteriorating, despite some maintenance by the MTC, for the next 61 years. It received a Grade 1 listing in the 1960s as only one of two such buildings in Lewisham (the other being St Paul, Deptford by Thomas Archer) and more recently was put on the EH's *'Buildings At Risk Register'*.

Building leases on the MTC's Belmont Estate, between Belmont Park and Blessington Road, expired in 1952. The 1876 Boone's almshouses and chapel on Lee High Road were sold to the Emmanuel Pentecostal Church in 1962. Religious fittings from the chapel were donated to other parishes in Cobham, Downham, Newington and Lee. Proceeds from this sale, and that of other land allowed the construction of 30 houses on Belmont Park, designed by William Holford architects (fig 36). At the time of writing the almshouses are likely to be rebuilt again with a new structure accommodating both the MTC and Boone's almshouse residents. If funding to pay for the building and to endow the charity is successful, 328 years of almshouse provision in the village of Lee will hopefully continue indefinitely - a fitting reflection of the foresight and charity of Christopher and Mary Boone.

34: top, interior of the second Boone's Chapel c1890
35: middle, drawing of the new Boone's almshouses 1876
36: bottom, typical house of the 1962 Boone's almshouses

37: left, Cowley's photograph of west elevation 1929
38: right, Cowley's photograph of the reading room 1929

39: the surviving fragments of the 1682 almshouses (see fig 19) ├─────────┤ 10cm

4 In the making

Design approach

Boone's Chapel is a single room of only 45 square metres. It is rectangular in plan with a projecting altar bay on the north side. The striking classically detailed exterior is in red brick with Portland stone dressings to the door surrounds, window architraves and it has rusticated quoins (blocks of stone at the corners). The roof is pyramidal and hipped with plain tiles, surmounted by an open wood cupola with leaded capping. The east, south and west elevations have triangular pediments with decorative carved cornices, also described as Corinthian modillions. The restoration strategy was to return the building to how it had been left in the 19th century, with the exception of modern services that would make the building usable as a studio space. The first part of this chapter explains the historic details and how the building was restored piece by piece.

The new service annexe, constructed to provide a kitchen and wc, is described on page 69. It was conceived as a separate building remote from the chapel with its front elevation treated as a new garden boundary. It assumes a low profile and was built in a contemporary style with environmental materials. It has a timber frame supporting a rain screen cladding made from the plain tiles reclaimed from the chapel roof.

The garden setting of the chapel with the large 17th century 'Zinnar' plane trees and the adjacent lawned quadrangle of the MTC almshouses was an important consideration at all stages of design and is described in more detail at the end of this chapter.

40: right, cut away isometric drawing of the chapel in its garden setting with the service building shown at the boundary wall; key:
a   original altar
b   physic garden
c   service annexe with recycled tile cladding
d   cupola
e   courtyard
f   front door (on open days)
g   woodland
h   hipped gable with carved cornice and modillions

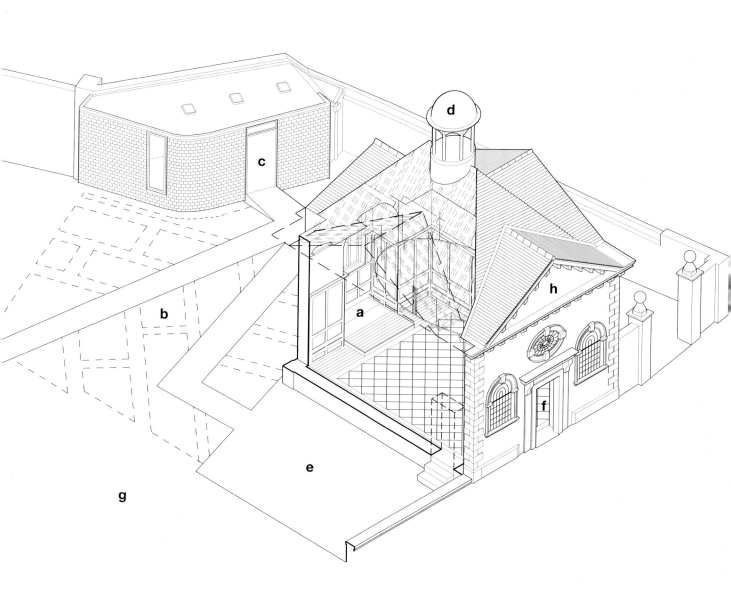

The chapel needed to be a flexible and adaptable space as it was primarily to be used as a studio. However, funding requirements for 30 public open days per year meant that it would need to be easily transformed into a public exhibition space. The original building lends itself well to a public use as the front doors open directly onto the main road right near a bus stop. Many visitors drop in while going about their day-to-day journeys and this means that the chapel benefits from a wide and diverse audience.

The regular transformation into a public space is facilitated by the adaptable design of the furniture and lighting. The desks incorporate trays, allowing small artefacts to be securely displayed underneath the glass desk tops. Office storage is housed in a gold painted mobile cube made of four components which, when open, holds 20 linear metres of shelving for files and printers. For exhibitions, the storage be arranged as a closed box, with four sides for hanging displays, or can be formed into a linear exhibition wall.

The idea was to return the chapel to its historic shell, installing as few fixed elements as possible. Instead of radiators, the chapel is heated with piped hot water under the floor. A modern minimal lighting track hung from the ceiling, provides adaptable lighting that can be directed towards the desks or at the display walls.

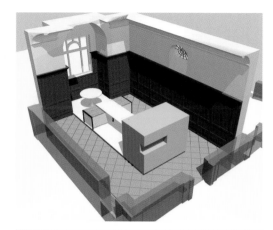

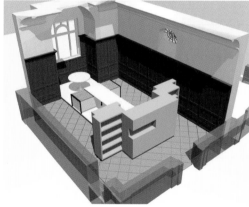

41: early interior concept drawing showing the chapel configured as an exhibition space (top) and as an office (bottom).

42: top, early design drawing showing the chapel and
    annexe in the garden
43: bottom, early design drawing showing the view of
    the new service annexe from the entrance gates.

Discoveries

The process of re-making the chapel began with detailed investigations of the historic fabric. The first priority was to understand the structural condition of the building. Every wall showed signs of settlement and the stone floor (covered by a 19th century timber floor) was sloped and bowed. Trial holes were commissioned to establish the condition of the foundations and, while digging near the altar end, local contractor Sean Schwegler noticed that a small section of the floor had collapsed into a hole. When he looked inside there were two coffins: he had discovered the burial vault containing Christopher and Mary Boone (fig 44). This was not entirely a surprise, as Mary's tomb had been described in local histories but with no evidence at ground level, the assumption had been there was no vault.

The vault and the coffins were examined by archaeologists from a firm called Pre Construct Archaeology (fig 45). While Christopher's coffin had deteriorated considerably, Mary's lay intact and was notable for its leather covering and brass studs. The chamber was recorded and the vault roof repaired and sealed leaving the burials undisturbed. With generous financial help from the MTC and the London Borough of Lewisham, the graves were finally marked with new memorial stones. These are described on page 62.

During the building works many artefacts were found revealing aspects of life in the 17th century. Many clay pipe bowls, dated to c1680, a time when tobacco was becoming common and pipe bowls were increasing in size, confirmed the historic sequence of works in the chapel. They were the cigarette stubs of their day. Other fragments found included glazed pottery, the leather sole of a shoe, and several animal bones, most likely left by workmen from their lunch (figs 47-49).

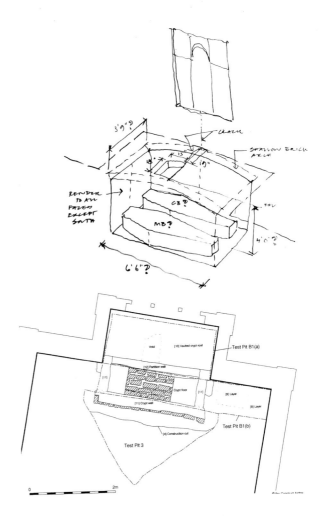

44: top, sketch explaining the vault for archaeologists
45: middle, archaeologists' report drawings
46: bottom, temporary commemoration left by Sean Schwegler

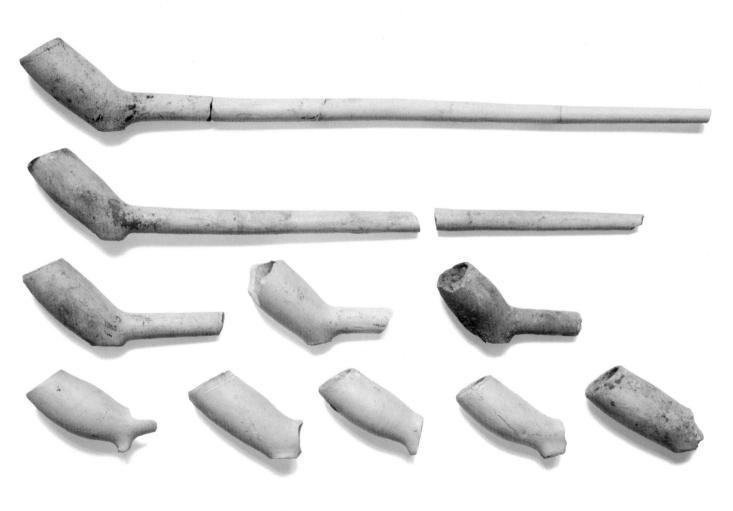

47: Clay pipe bowls dated by the archaeologists as being c1680 ⊢————⊣2cm

49

48: objects from under the floor left at construction c1682: left, a broken shoe; top, broken utensils; above broken pottery ⊢———⊣ 2cm

49: objects from nineteenth century works: left, a bottle left during
underpinning; right, a newspaper filling a gap in the altar window

├────┤ 2cm

Conservation team

The plans for restoring the chapel began several years before the actual works started on site. Every element of work had to be drawn and described and costed, and a sequence for operations on site had to be devised and tested well in advance. All elements of the repairs were developed by Research Design with Stephen Rickards, a building surveyor accredited in conservation, who was the contract administrator for the project. Local structural engineers, Brian Pawsey and Peter Thake of John Mason and Partner, were involved at all stages, helping develop practical solutions to stabilise the building. The team also benefited from the experience of Terry Doyle, of Foresight, who assisted with the programme development, and Gordon MacKeith who advised on health and safety matters.

Numerous highly skilled and experienced crafts people were also consulted as part of the design process. Emma Simpson, a well known brick specialist generously gave advice on the cleaning and repairing of the brickwork. Stone and plaster specialists were also consulted. This wealth of experience was essential in developing a 'light touch' approach to the restoration of the building. The intention was to conserve it with all its traces of 17th century and Victorian history intact. The tender for the main contract was won by HJ Johnston and Son Ltd of Chiddingstone Causeway in Kent, and the eleven month programme of works finally began in November 2007. The work comprised three distinct packages: repairs to the historic fabric, the conversion elements including new services for the chapel and the building of the stand alone service building and the garden.

The chapel repairs were carried out to all elements of the building, including the foundations, the stone and brickwork, the roof and ceiling, the floor, the plasterwork, and the windows and doors. The budget for the project was £450,000 and the proposals were costed by the quantity surveyor Glynne Procter of the Tom Lucas Partnership, for approval by the BHBT. All repairs also needed approval from the local authority conservation officer and EH. Finally there was a programme to halt the deterioration of the building and preserve it for the next 350 years. It would involve a great deal of work and managing time and prioritising costs was critical. In order to restore and conserve the building, it would have to be stripped back to its basic structure.

50: first stage of the building works Spring 2008: scaffold and enclose the existing structure

Stabilising the building

Excavation revealed that the chapel had been underpinned along three sides but not under the vault. The diagram in figure 51 shows how the building had moved over time causing large cracks in the walls and ceiling and bowing in the floor. Soil investigations revealed that the clay soil was desiccated, meaning that its structure had broken down and it had shrunk in volume. This was probably due to the proximity of the large trees. The structural engineers determined that the altar end would need to be underpinned using barrel loads of new concrete to support the brick walls. This was carefully carried out in incremental sections. The vault was also repaired leaving the coffins undisturbed. Over 150 helibars were needed to repair the large vertical cracks in the brick walls (figures 51, 52). Helibars are stainless steel rods that are set within the mortar joints and then repointed. New bricks were chosen to match both inside and out but brick replacement was limited to those with severe cracking.

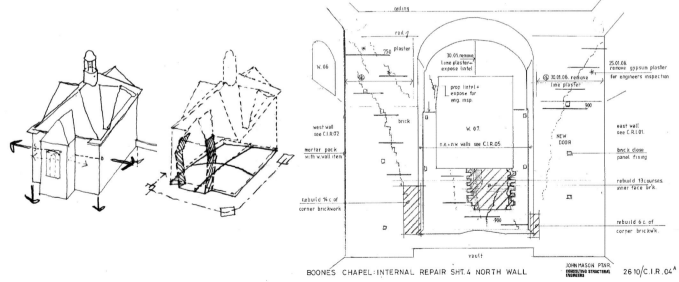

BOONES CHAPEL: INTERNAL REPAIR SHT. 4 NORTH WALL

JOHN MASON PTNR.
CONSULTING STRUCTURAL ENGINEERS

26 10/C.I.R.04 A

51: top, exposed friable and cracked brickwork
52: left, diagrammatic analysis, right, crack repair proposals

Roof repairs

The building had been re-roofed in the 1970s but there had been extensive water damage to the interior. All the roof tiles needed to be removed from the chapel roof so that the timbers could be inspected and repaired. Most of the tiles were salvaged and carefully stacked for use in cladding the service building. It was decided that new tiles should be used on the chapel roof to ensure a longer life. Many samples were examined to find the best match to the historic tiles. Kent bonnet hips, a special curved corner tile, were used to make neater corners to the gables. Many of the exposed roof timbers were original 17th century oak members. Several of them have the distinctive joiner's marks carved in. Spliced repairs were needed to three of the four corners of the structure which had rotted so badly that the roof was on the brink of failure. The splicing was skilfully carried out with all the oak members in situ. The cupola with its timber structure and lead capping was extensively repaired by skilled joiners and lead workers.

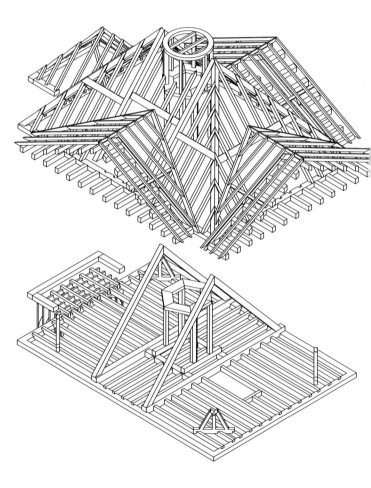

53: top, the cupola
54: bottom, typical valley and gutter

55: roof survey drawing
top, roof timbers, bottom, ceiling joists and trusses

56: exposed roof timbers seen from below,
March 2008

57: top, roof over altar bay and arch
58: bottom, typical spliced timber repair in oak

59: left top, comparison of old and new tiles
60: left bottom, production of tiles at Keymer's factory
61: above, new leadwork gutter and preparation of roof,
    northwest corner, April 2008

62: left, re-tiling the south pediment and valley junction with main
roof, April 2008

63: above, the roof completed: the curved corner tiles are called
Kent bonnet hips, May 2008

Floor and wall repairs

In its new use the space would need to be heated. The walls were all very damp already and heating the space was likely to make things worse. Like many historic buildings the chapel does not have a damp proof course, meaning that there was no moisture-proof barrier to prevent damp from entering the walls and floor. Historically, this would have been a manageable problem, as the draughty windows and doors would keep a good flow of air to ventilate the space. The building would also not have had any heating until gas fired radiators were installed in the Victorian period.

It was decided to install a new modern dampproof barrier to prevent the restored structure from becoming damp, and this was done with tanking under the floor and up to window cill height forming a bath-like liner to protect the main space. This barrier prevents moisture from being drawn up through the new stone floor, and is ventilated at its sides behind the reinstated oak panelling. This means that the walls and floor are still able to breathe. The system was approved by EH who favour removable systems. The new floor system required a new concrete slab to be cast and thick insulation to conserve heat. This involved digging out almost half a metre of earth. The archaeologist identified that, apart from the front which had been underpinned in the Victorian period, and the vault area, the earth was 'virgin' soil, meaning that no further burials or vaults would be discovered.

64: above, view looking south after removal of stone floor exposing earth base November 2007
65: right, view looking south with new concrete subfloor and heating with breathable tanking, May 2008
66: far right, view looking north with new door, May 2008

Brick and stone repairs

Brick work repairs had been carried out to the exterior of the chapel at many stages over the past three centuries resulting in a mixture of brick colours and mortar types. At one stage, possibly the 19th century, the entire building was sooted (daubed with soot solution to darken the brickwork), and it was this rather than traffic pollution that gave the chapel its distinctively dark south elevation. The decision was reached to clean the building lightly, to remove some of the acidic pollution from its surface, but not so that the numerous different coloured bricks would be exposed.

Large vertical cracks to the west and north sides were repaired by cutting out the bricks and inserting new ones (fig 67). These areas of repairs were lightly sooted to tone them in with the adjacent weathered bricks.

Four different types of brick were found to match the different types on each of the facades. New bricks were custom-fired by specialist Tony Minter of Bulmer Brick and Tile, in the traditional brick kilns still found at their premises in Suffolk. Large areas of hard cement pointing had to be retained because removing it damaged the arrises (or edges) of the bricks. Where it was possible to rake back the joints, a blackened mortar was used for repointing to match the street frontage.

The decorative stone quoins (or corner blocks) and window cills to the front had cracked due to building movement and were badly damaged by damp, salt and pollution from the main road. Carved sections were replaced with Portland stone to match the original. Other stone details including the window and front door surrounds were in reasonable condition and were lightly cleaned.

67: top left, removing cracked bricks by hand; right, matching new to existing
68: bottom left, repairs to stone quoins; right, completed repairs to south window

The new brick door

A new doorway was added at the north of the chapel to give access to the service building at the rear. As a contemporary addition the door has a modern design, but it was conceived in the spirit of a traditional 'jib' door, which is hidden or camouflaged with the wall it is set in. Externally it is clad with bricks using modern adhesives and hinges. Internally a second door was made from the oak panelling. The 45cm depth of wall between the two openings accommodates all the building's switches and controls.

69: left, removal of bricks to allow structural repairs to northeast corner
70: middle, new stainless steel frame and door with bonded handmade slip bricks
71: right, completed door with folded steel plate stair

The new stone floor

Before restoration the floor was partially covered by a 19th century timber floor. When it was uncovered it was found to be made of Purbeck Downsvein stone. Several flags were missing and the top of the stone had badly de-laminated (fig 1). The whole floor surface was sloped, and bowed. The diagonal square arrangement of stone flags is known as a '*Mitchell*' pattern. The decision was reached with EH and the local conservation team to replace the stone with new to the original pattern. The new stone was quarried at Haysom's quarry at Worth Matravers in Dorset, still owned by the same family who supplied the original stone to the chapel. The stone is formed of compacted shells from the lagoon bed.

All evidence of the altar floor had been lost so a new oak step was made over the vault and the burials were marked with two hand carved slabs of Purbeck Green marble. The lettering was designed with the help of inscription expert Annette Stirling who helped develop the typography with reference to other 17th century examples.

73: left, processing quarried blocks at Haysom's Quarry, April 2008
72: top, samples to identify the quarry and matching stones
74: above left, preparing the memorial stones in green 'marble'
75: above right, the completed stones in place

76: shark's dorsal fin bone dating from the Cretaceous period approximately ⊢———⊣ 2cm
140 million years old, found in blocks at the quarry used for the floor

Plasterwork repairs

Most of the ornate plaster work dates back to the 1870s when the west wall was completely re-built after the demolition of the adjoining almshouses. Above the altar is a finely decorated arch which could date back to the 17th century. The lath and plaster arch is suspended from an oak frame concealed in the roof. Several of these timbers had extensive dry rot. They were treated and reinforced. The historic plaster details were fully conserved. Details include cherub heads, fruit and foliage including hops, foxgloves, roses and pears. The four Victorian cherubs' heads had to be replicated by recasting from fragments of the originals.

77: left, dry rot was found above the ornate altar vault
78: top, re-forming the plaster cove and ceiling
79: bottom, reinstalled angel head and wings

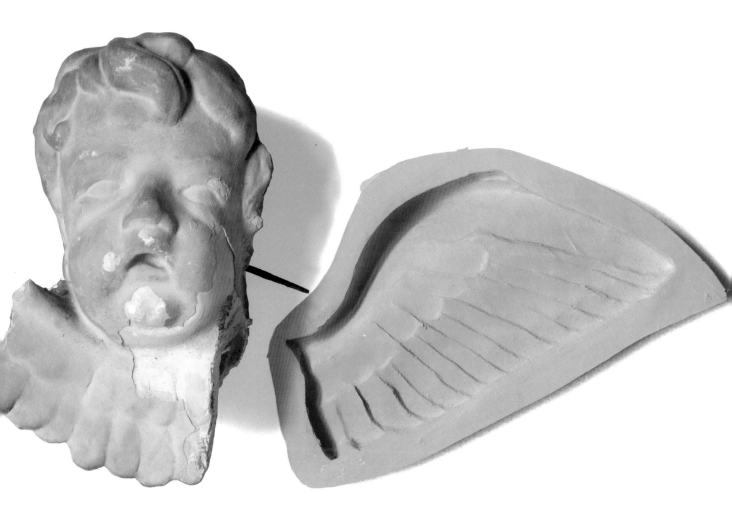

80: reclaimed fragment of angel head and new wing mould ├────── ─────┤ 5cm

Decorative timber repairs

Boone's Chapel has very distinctive carved timber details below the cornice and under the gable eaves. This classical detail is known as a modillion.

The paint was removed to reveal fine carved oak designs based on scrolled acanthus leaves. The design is identical to that seen on the nearby gazebo at the Grange on Crooms Hill attributed to Robert Hooke (fig 21). Several of the modillions were rotten with repairs being carried out with resin that could be sculpted to recreate the design. This method meant that the original fabric could be retained where possible.

The nineteenth century fielded oak panelling and the oak panelled doors were carefully labelled and taken down for restoring at the HJ Johnston workshop in Chiddingstone Causeway (fig 84). They were badly water damaged and wet rot and wood worm were prevalent. The timber was cleaned with wire wool and rubbed down with bees wax. Some sections had to be replaced or spliced with new oak that was pigmented and polished to match. The oak doors were repaired with carefully pigmented resin, which meant that as much original timber could be retained as possible.

After cleaning and re-waxing the panels were reinstated. New brackets and continuous fixing rails for hanging drawings or artwork were installed behind the original panelling cornice to so that displays could be created without having to fix into the panelling.

81: top, cornice modillions before removal of paint
82: middle, resin repairs to preserve original timber
83: completed repairs

84: top left, existing panelling after cleaning by hand; compare with fig 7
85: top right, installing repaired panelling
86: bottom left, spliced repairs in oak to original west door
87: bottom right, repaired lock mechanism

Replacement windows

The chapel has five elliptical leaded windows and a north facing Serlian window. Much of the original glass was missing and the frames were damaged. Historic photographs showed an opening window to the west side with the elliptical frame rotating on a central hinge. Two new windows were made with this mechanism, by Don Barker's company of blacksmiths using salvaged glass to maintain the historic appearance. Externally the stone surrounds with distinctive carved stone volutes only needed to be lightly cleaned.

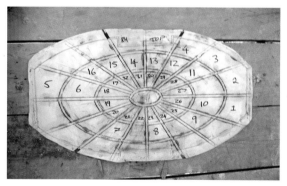

88: top left, reclaimed leading and glass from surviving windows
89: bottom left, blacksmith's patterns for new leading
90: above, completed window with reinstated 'tilt turn'

The new annexe

The 16 square metre service building was constructed against the brick garden boundary wall. Its unusual geometry responds to the height and angle of this wall, with the curved front elevation designed so that the sight lines would be maintained between the chapel and the almshouses.

The annexe is clad in reclaimed weathered plain tiles from the chapel roof. Although the building is brand new, the material of its exterior is old, and this meant that the building immediately fitted in with the chapel. The building functions practically as a kitchen and toilet and it houses the boiler for the chapel's underfloor heating. The interior is lined with ply wood and it has yacht hatches as roof lights. Windows were positioned to give views of the garden, but all details were designed with security in mind. The space is compact and so a custom designed kitchen counter and shelving were essential to make the space work. The space has full height library shelving and is used for meetings, team lunches and extra studio space.

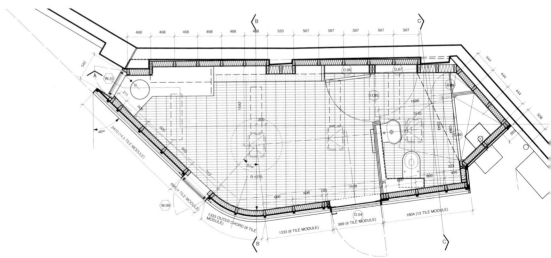

91: top, timber shell of annexe, April 2008
92: middle, cladding the annexe with reclaimed tiles
93: bottom, working drawing of annexe plan

69

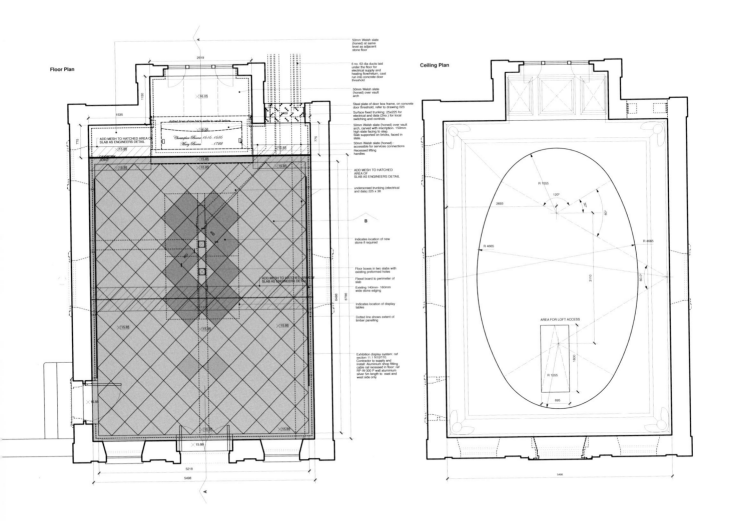

Completion

Floor Plan

Ceiling Plan

94: working drawing plans of chapel: left, floor plan; right, reflected ceiling plan

95: interior looking south,
October 2008

96: interior looking west in office use,
October 2008

97. interior looking north in office use,
October 2008

98: interior: new doors open,
October 2008

99: annexe and chapel,
October 2008

100: almshouses and annexe, October 2008

101: annexe and paths, October 2008

102: annexe interior, October 2008

103: annexe interior, October 2008

Boone's Chapel

104: the doors about to be opened for the first public visits,
Open House London, September 2008

The garden

The chapel has an area of garden within its lease boundary of approximately 300 square metres. Any landscaping of this would need to maintain clear views of the chapel, using low level planting and no fences or walls. However, there was the opportunity to make the garden a space in itself that would attract visitors and provide interest.

The garden design (fig 105) was conceived as a contemporary interpretation of the almshouse residents' gardens described in a 1683 indenture. A large area of gravel to the west side provides a gathering space next to the chapel, while the rest is intensively laid out as a 'physic' garden with medicinal plants and herbs inspired by medieval pottager gardens and the well known physic garden at Chelsea.

The garden at Chelsea was founded just before the chapel in 1673, as an Apothecary's garden or *hortus catalogii*. Many of the plants were brought back from India, Africa and the Far East by trading merchants like Christopher Boone. As with Chelsea, the Boone's Chapel physic garden has educational aspirations. The initial planting was started by a group of local school children and interpretation of the plants and activities are planned for the future.

A lattice of cockleshell plantsman's paths and hoggin walkways is edged with more of the chapel's recycled roof tiles. The cockleshells came from the trawlermen's cockle sheds at Leigh-on-Sea in Essex.

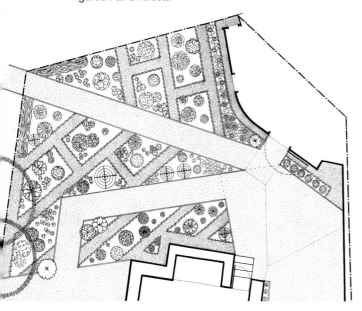

105: above, planting plan for the chapel garden
106: right, planting day with 12 local children

107: Pat Appleton and Ron Fraser, two of the residents of the
MTC almshouses who walk through the physic garden daily

108: above, poppies collected from Barrow-in-Furness, Cumbria
109: right, salads and vegetables in beds marked by reclaimed tiles

110: above, the newly established border, August 2008
111: right, beds established, May 2010

112: beds established, May 2010

113: tulip, May 2009

Open days and exhibitions

The first open weekend for Boone's Chapel was held on London Open House Weekend September 2008. There have been nearly 4,300 visitors through the doors in our first 65 open days. Most visitors have been local and desperate to see inside a building they pass daily.

The resident architectural practice, Research Design, has established the venue as a local space for regularly changing exhibitions. The practice curates its own series of themed exhibitions about architecture and design, as well as collaborating with local and international artists, and local groups. The first exhibition entitled '*Boone's Chapel - history in the making*' inspired this book. The following pages describe some of the exhibitions displayed since September 2008.

114: left, local newspaper announcement of completion
115: above left and right, the first open day

Boone's Chapel - history in the making
September - December 2008

The first exhibition to mark the re-opening of the building described the chapel's history using historic photographs, drawings and artefacts discovered during the building works. The story of the repairs and alterations was accompanied by a video, which explained the process of restoration and included several interviews with local people and almshouse residents.

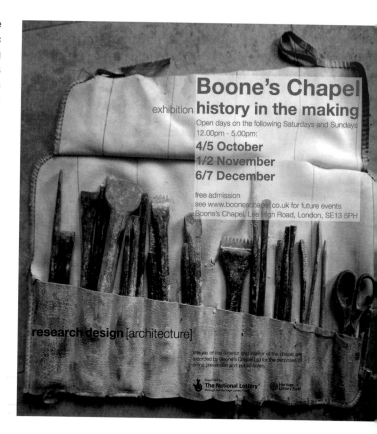

116: left, exhibition visitors
117: right, poster for first exhibition showing a mason's tool bag

useful beauty #1: Traps
January - February 2009

The second exhibition displayed our collection of traps from around the world. It illustrated how a common task - to catch a mouse - can lead to many innovative and diverse design solutions. Every year 400 patents for mousetraps designs are submitted worldwide. This is just one example of an everyday object that many people have felt inspired to design and make in their own way.

useful beauty #2: Drawing Tools
March - May 2009

A number of collections of drawing tools from the last three centuries were displayed, together with drawings to demonstrate how the tools were used. The exhibition explored the relationship between drawing techniques and the resulting designs, comparing Pencil and Pen Aided Design (PAD) with Computer Aided Design (CAD).

lefthand page clockwise from top left:
118: 'kill' trap, Spanish collected 1993
119: 'collect' trap, French collected 2008
120: 'collect' trap, Dutch collected 2005
121: 'kill' trap, Finnish collected 2000
this page
122: early eighteenth century drawing instruments

architectures #1: The 21st century almshouse
May - June 2009

Providing suitable housing for older people is one of the biggest issues facing society today. The most asked questions by visitors are about the idyllic setting of the MTC almshouses. Therefore, this exhibition was inspired by the historic and present day almshouse context of Boone's Chapel. It explained what almshouses are and why they were built. The exhibition used local, national and international examples to explain the different building forms and details which make them good places to live, and a viable model for new sustainable communities. Both contemporary and historic case studies were included in the exhibition, as well as video interviews with current residents of the MTC almshouses.

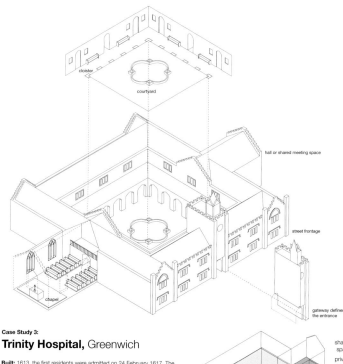

cloister
courtyard
hall or shared meeting space
street frontage
chapel
gateway defines the entrance

Case Study 3:

Trinity Hospital, Greenwich

Built: 1613, the first residents were admitted on 24 February 1617, The hospital was rebuilt in 1812 in its present Gothic style and is still in use.
Founder: by Henry Howard, Earl of Northampton
Howard stipulated there were to be twelve spaces offered to local men and eight spaces given to men from Howards birthplace in Shottesham, Norfolk. He also made it clear in his statute that,

'the resident shall be a man that is decayed, and is become poor by casual means, and not through his own dissolute life, and one that hath always lived in honest name. No common beggar, drunkard, whore-hunter, haunter of taverns nor ale houses nor unclean person infected with any foul disease, nor any that is blind, or so impotent as he is not able, at the time of his admission to come to prayers daily . . . nor any idiot, nor any other that is not able to say, without book, the Lord's Prayer, the Creed and the Ten Commandments.'

shared space
private space

Diagram showing spaces
the g

123: one of a series of diagrams explaining almshouse types by Madeleine Adams and Rosie Hervey

non almshouse design elements

d space

entrances

gateways

paths and routes

living in an almshouse

rules

inside

furniture

dress

haarlem

Parallels with the UK:

124: top, summary of the 'ingredients' of almshouses

125: bottom, historic almshouse in the centre of Leiden, Holland

126: extension to the fourteenth century Johannes Enschede Hofje
      (almshouses) by Henk Döll architects with Joost Schwarte, 2007

collaborations #1: Run for it!
December 2009

An Age Exchange exhibition of collected memories of sport and play from the 1940s, 50s and 60s. The exhibition included old toys, children's descriptions of games and John Drysdale's photographs from the 1950s. Older people's stories were recorded during reminiscence afternoons in care settings and workshops for local school children contrasted attitudes to play then and now. The chapel and the exhibition were used by the Age Exchange Youth Theatre for their workshops while devising a play performing these memories at the Bakehouse Theatre in Blackheath.

" It was not a throwaway society then: everything was recycled and re-used" Gordon

play & war

127: left, 'Jacks' being demonstrated
128: above, one of eight panels produced to summarise reminiscences of childhood

collaborations #2: The Churches Conservation Trust
September - November 2009

Archaeologist Dr Neil Rushton and Rebecca Rees of the Churches Conservation Trust (CCT), organised an exhibition celebrating the trust's successful conservation projects over the last 40 years. The exhibition included historic artefacts from current church projects as well as black and white photographs by acclaimed photographer Christopher Dalton.

collaborations #4: Making do
February - March 2010

Boone's Chapel and Age Exchange presented an exhibition of reminiscence artefacts to trigger visitors memories about daily life in the 1940s, 50s, 60s and 70s. The '*Make do and Mend*' principle and what can be made or recycled in the garden shed is familiar to the older generation. The project will be developed by Age Exchange throughout 2010, as one of their reminiscence arts projects in care settings and schools.

129: top, visitors to the Churches Conservation Trust exhibition
130: bottom, poster for 'making do' exhibition

collaborations #3: Care
January 2010

Boone's Chapel was one of several venues across London which hosted this exhibition presented by Age Exchange. The 6 month reminiscence project funded by the Arts Council England, involved working with older people, carers and health care professionals. It explored the issue of care for older people across the generations resulting in works by artists Tanya Kaprielian (figs 131, 132) and Tim Sutton (figs 132-135). The exhibition included photographs, narrative text pieces and drawings and interactive sound pieces as well as projection of filmed interviews on the ceiling of the chapel.

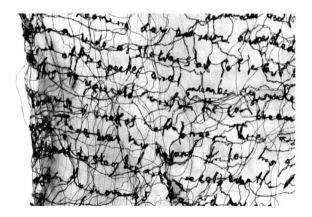

131: *I do love a rose*
narrative text (2009)

132: Kaprielian's *I do love a rose* in context with Sutton's *Some of the older people I have met and talked to*, 50 digital portraits (2009)

133: top, *Reading between the lines*
a series of 5 short films (2009)
134: bottom, *Sound Affects*,
audio installation re-using a Dolls
Eye switchboard c.1960 (2009)

135: *Miss Stepney 1954*
lightjet metallic print on aluminium (2009)

The Lee Heritage Trail

The chapel lies on the local Lee Heritage Trail, which was initiated by the BHBT in 2008 to carry on the heritage work started at Boone's Chapel. The trail starts in the old churchyard of St Margaret's at the top of Brandram Road and tells the story of Lee, with individual enamel panels marking the sites of the three churches which have served the parish since the 12th century, two large local manor houses, the chapel and the MTC almshouses, and a surviving Ice house at Manor House Gardens. The panels not only reveal the fragments of history that survived suburbanisation but increase support for future repair projects. The first panel has led to the restoration of the fifteenth century fabric of the first parish church ruin, due for completion in September 2010.

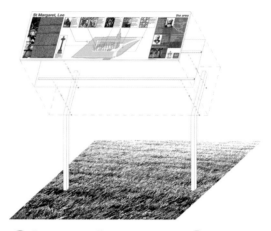

Old Churchyard St Margar

For almost a 1000 years this churchyard has been a focal point in the area. The tower, which has stood for eight centuries, is all that remains of earlier churches. Bells have summoned generations to worship and may have encouraged Jack Cade and his Kentish rebels to kneel in prayer on Blackheath before marching to London in 1450. Babies were brought here for baptism, lovers came here to plight their troth and funeral rites were read prior to burial in the hallowed turf. It is estimated that over 5,000 have been interred here.

Three 18th century Astronomers Royal are buried here. The best known, Edmond Halley is buried beneath a chest tomb near the east wall. Halley's Comet is named after him. John Pond is buried in the same vault and Nathaniel Bliss lies in an unmarked grave.

Adjacent to the tower is the mausoleum of the family of Christopher Boone, the founder of the almshouses which bear his name. Others interred here include Sir Samuel Fludyer, Lord Mayor of London in 1761, the eighteenth Baron Dacre, Sir John Call and Robert Cocking, an early aeronaut who in 1837 fell to his death in a local field when his primitive parachute failed. The gravestones of more humble folk display stonemasons' craft depicting bell, book and candle and skull and crossbones.

The tower was listed in 1954. In recognition of the national importance of the churchyard, 23 tombs and monuments were listed in 2007. The Fludyer [14] and Call [257] tombs are listed Grade 2*. The 23 tombs are shown on the plan as well as some of the stories of the countless people buried here.

The main drawing shows the churchyard as seen from Lee Terrace. The numbers indicate marked graves and are taken from Edwyn and Josephine Birchenough's book 'Tombstones at Old Churchyard, St. Margaret's Church, Lee', 1967, in Lewisham library.

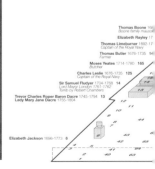

Lady Dacre — Wife of Baron Dacre — 13

Lady Dacre commissioned her husband's tomb (to the left in the drawing). A servant was given a bequest of £40 to clean the tomb every week.

[LLHC]

Thomas Boone 16 *Boone family mausoleum*
Elizabeth Rayley 17
Thomas Limeburner 1692-17 *Captain of the Royal Navy*
Thomas Butler 1676-1735 14 *Farmer*
Moses Yeates 1714-1780 165 *Butcher*
Charles Leslie 1676-1735 125 *Captain of the Royal Navy*
Sir Samuel Fludyer 1704-1768 14 *Lord Mayor London 1761-1762 / Tomb by Robert Chambers*
Trevor Charles Roper Baron Dacre 1745-1794 13
Lady Mary Jane Dacre 1755-1804
Elizabeth Jackson 1696-1773 6

136: far left, MTC almshouse panel installed 2008
137: left, panels are read daily
138: bottom, old churchyard panel installed 2007
139: top, diagram of panel assembly

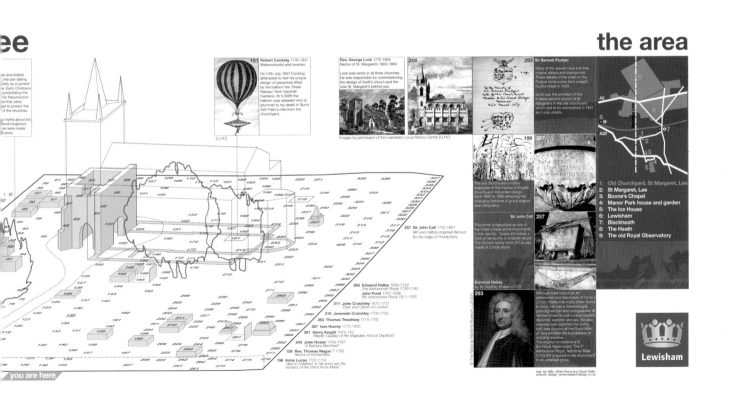

ee

the area

ee associated
ural pre-dating
sibly as a symbol
er. Early Christians
symbolising the
he Resurrection.
ed that yews
o to protect the
of the churches.

e myths about the
eval longbows,
es were made
l yews.

191 **Robert Cocking** 1776-1837
Watercolourist and inventor.

On 24th July 1837 Cocking
attempted to test his unique
design of parachute lifted
by the balloon the 'Great
Nassau' from Vauxhall
Gardens. At 5,000ft the
balloon was released only to
plummet to his death in Burnt
Ash Field a mile from the
churchyard.

[LLHC]

Rev. George Lock 1770-1864 **218**
Rector of St. Margaret's 1803-1864

Lock was rector in all three churches.
He was responsible for commissioning the
design of Gwilt's church and the
new St. Margaret's behind you.

Images by permission of the Lewisham Local History Centre [LLHC]

293 **Sir Samuel Fludyer**

Many of the graves have lost their
original details and inscriptions.
These details of the crest on the
Fludyer tomb come from Joseph
Gwilt's notes in 1830.

Gwilt was the architect of the
ill fated second church of St
Margaret's in the old churchyard
which had to be demolished in 1841
as it was unsafe.

The old churchyard contains
examples of the heyday of English
churchyard monument design
from 1680 to 1830 reflecting the
changing fashions of grave shapes
and calligraphy. **199** **257**

Sir John Call **257**

This tomb is described as one of
the finest Coade stone monuments
in the country. Coade still makes a
form of terracotta to a secret recipe.
The Chivers family tomb [57] is also
made of Coade stone.

257 **Sir John Call** 1732-1801
MP and military engineer famous
for the siege of Pondicherry

Edmond Halley 1656-1721
by Sir Godfrey Kneller c.1721 **293**

293 **Edmond Halley** 1656-1742
2nd Astronomer Royal 1720-1742
John Pond 1767-1836
6th Astronomer Royal 1811-1835

211 **John Crutchley** 1675-1727
'Dyer and Citizen of London'

210 **Jeremiah Crutchley** 1709-1752

283 **Thomas Treadway** 1714-1780

267 **Ives Hurrey** 1773-1800

281 **Henry Knight** 1675-142
'Master Caulker of His Majesties Yard at Deptford'

243 **John Hosier** 1706-1767
'A Barbary Merchant'

159 **Rev. Thomas Megus** ?-1765
Rector of Rotherhithe

198 **Anne Lucas** 1722-1758
'died in childbed, in her arms are the
remains of her infant Anna Maria'

Although best known as an
astronomer and discoverer of Halley's
Comet, Halley has many other claims
to fame. He was a meteorologist
geomagnetician and cartographer. At
various times he was a naval captain,
diplomat, explorer and spy. He also
invented and exploited the diving
bell, was director of the Royal Mint
at York and laid the foundations of
actuarial science.
The original tombstone is in
the Royal Observatory. The 4th
Astronomer Royal, Nathaniel Bliss
(1700-64) is buried in the churchyard
in an unmarked grave.

1: Old Churchyard, St Margaret, Lee
2: St Margaret, Lee
3: Boone's Chapel
4: Manor Park house and garden
5: The Ice House
6: Lewisham
7: Blackheath
8: The Heath
9: The old Royal Observatory

Lewisham

you are here

text: Ian Mills, Alfred Wood and Stuart Malin
artwork, design: www.researchdesign.co.uk

© The National Maritime Museum, London

5 Appendices

Materials

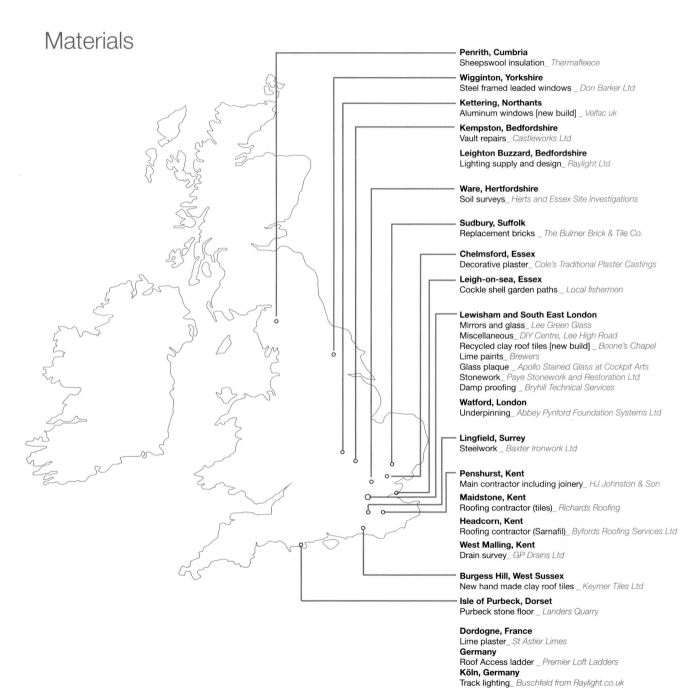

Penrith, Cumbria
Sheepswool insulation_ *Thermafleece*

Wigginton, Yorkshire
Steel framed leaded windows _ *Don Barker Ltd*

Kettering, Northants
Aluminum windows [new build] _ *Velfac uk*

Kempston, Bedfordshire
Vault repairs_ *Castleworks Ltd*

Leighton Buzzard, Bedfordshire
Lighting supply and design_ *Raylight Ltd*

Ware, Hertfordshire
Soil surveys_ *Herts and Essex Site Investigations*

Sudbury, Suffolk
Replacement bricks _ *The Bulmer Brick & Tile Co.*

Chelmsford, Essex
Decorative plaster_ *Cole's Traditional Plaster Castings*

Leigh-on-sea, Essex
Cockle shell garden paths _ *Local fishermen*

Lewisham and South East London
Mirrors and glass_ *Lee Green Glass*
Miscellaneous_ *DIY Centre, Lee High Road*
Recycled clay roof tiles [new build] _ *Boone's Chapel*
Lime paints_ *Brewers*
Glass plaque _ *Apollo Stained Glass at Cockpit Arts*
Stonework_ *Paye Stonework and Restoration Ltd*
Damp proofing _ *Bryhill Technical Services*

Watford, London
Underpinning_ *Abbey Pynford Foundation Systems Ltd*

Lingfield, Surrey
Steelwork _ *Baxter Ironwork Ltd*

Penshurst, Kent
Main contractor including joinery_ *HJ Johnston & Son*

Maidstone, Kent
Roofing contractor (tiles)_ *Richards Roofing*

Headcorn, Kent
Roofing contractor (Sarnafil)_ *Byfords Roofing Services Ltd*

West Malling, Kent
Drain survey_ *GP Drains Ltd*

Burgess Hill, West Sussex
New hand made clay roof tiles _ *Keymer Tiles Ltd*

Isle of Purbeck, Dorset
Purbeck stone floor _ *Landers Quarry*

Dordogne, France
Lime plaster_ *St Astier Limes*
Germany
Roof Access ladder _ *Premier Loft Ladders*
Köln, Germany
Track lighting_ *Buschfeld from Raylight.co.uk*

Illustration credits

Photography © Tim Crocker (www.timcrocker.co.uk) September 2007: figures cover, 1, 6-12; September 2008-February 2009: figures 95-104, 107, 140

Illustrations and photography © Boone's Chapel: figures 2, 16, 18, 20, 21, 23, 27, 36, 39, 47-49, 76, 80, 105, 106, 108-121, 123-126, 129, 136-139

Illustrations and photography © Research Design Architecture: figures 3, 4, 40-44, 46, 50, 51, 53-73, 75, 77-79, 81-94

Illustration © Niall Phillips Architects: figure 5

Illustrations courtesy of Alfred Wood: figures 13, 14, 28, 29, 35

Illustrations by kind permission of the Merchant Taylors' Company and the Corporation of London: figures (photography by Gordon and Margaret MacKeith) 15, (photography by Boone's Chapel) figures 17, 30, 32

Illustrations by kind permission of Lewisham Local History Centre: figures 19, 24, 26, 31, 33, 34, 37, 38

Illustration from B+T Langley's 'The Builder's Jewel' 1749: figure 22

Illustrations courtesy of Ian Mills: figure 25

Illustrations and photography © Landers Haysoms Quarry: figure 74

Illustration © Pre-Construct Archaeology: figure 45

Illustration © John Mason and Partner: figure 52

Illustration by permission of Gordon MacKeith, photography © Boone's Chapel: figure 122

Illustration © Age Exchange: figure (photography Boone's Chapel) 127, 128, 130, 132, (photography Tanya Kaprielian) 131, (photography Tim Sutton) 133-135

Transcript of 1683 Indenture and Schedule on front and rear cover pages and following taken from counsel's transcripts c.1858 by kind permission of the Merchant Taylors' Company and the Corporation of London

Acknowledgements

This project was funded by

The Heritage Lottery Fund
Gordon and Margaret MacKeith
English Heritage
London Borough of Lewisham
The Merchant Taylors' Company
Other City of London Livery Companies
Countless local people

Client

The Blackheath Historic Buildings Trust
Sir Ian Mills (Chair 2003-)
Sir Geoffrey Chipperfield (Chair 1999-2003)
Julia Maynard (2004-)
Tim Barnes QC (1999-)
Charles Batchelor (1999-)
Penny Jonas (1999-2007)
Sir David Nicholas (1999-2008)

Contract administration
Architecture and design

Structural engineering
Quantity Surveyor
Project Management
CDM Co-ordinator
Contractor

Stephen Rickards (Rickards Conservation)
Madeleine Adams, Fran Balaam, Rosie Hervey,
Charlie MacKeith (Research Design)
Brian Pawsey, Peter Thake (John Mason & Partner)
Glynne Procter (The Tom Lucas Partnership)
Terry Doyle (Foresight Project Support)
Gordon MacKeith (MacKeith Dickinson & Partners)
Stephen Johnston, David Macmillan and Malcolm
Osborne with Graham Baxter, Anthony Bourne, Mick
Croucher, John Dunlop, Jason Farrington, Andrew
Greenaway, Brian Hemsley, Mark Hemsley, Mark
Hibbett, Ian Hollamby, Julian Hynes, Tom Jones, Des
Kirby, Latham Kirby, Vince Palmer, David Pilbeam,
Robert Pullman, David Sayers, Jack Southwart,
Anthony Thomas, Tony Turnerm, Kevin Weyman
(HJ Johnston & Son Ltd)

We wish to thank all the following people who have helped this project

Martyn Adams, Sam Adams, Phil Ashford, Trish Barnes, Stuart Bastik, John Bayford, Alli Beddoes, Tristram Besterman, John Bevan, Marcus Binney, Neil Bingham, Bob Boone, Ray Brookes, June Broome, Mike Bullen, Steve Bullock, Gary Capstick, Harry Charrington, Nick Collins, Morris Coxall, John Coulter, Chris and Liz Crane, Bill Dunn, Nicholas Cranfield, Matthew Davies, Kerry Downes, Ann Doyle, Gabriella, Imogen and Marlene Drew, Nancy Elliot, Lorraine Elliott, Susan Field, Simon Flowerdew, Stephen Freeth, William Fuller, Bobby Furber, Nigel Gammon, David Gatliffe, Anthony Geraghty, Joshua and Sarah Gibbs, Peter Guillery, Chris Hare, Nick Harris, Steve Harris, Trev Haysom, Ron Hearn, William Hervey, Ray Hewitt, Peter Horton, Adrian, Angelina, Melissa, Paola and Paola Hoy, Matthew Hunter, Ralph Hyde, Tanya Kaprielian, John King, Alex Knights, Suzanne Lockett, Malachy McAleer, Grace MacKeith, James and Marge MacKeith, Prof Margaret MacKeith, Chris Mayo, Elizabeth Mills, Jan Mondrzejewski, Tony Minter, John and Suzanne Mockett, Frances Muir, Evie, Nancy and Neds Netherwood, Paul Newsam, Justine Page, Ray Pampling, John Payne Estate Agents, Olwen and Richard Pearson, John Penton, Beryl Platts, Claire Pollock, Janie Price, Simon Purins, Rebecca Rees, Neil Rhind, Diana Rimmel, Neil Rushton, Frank Salmon, Ann Saunders, Renie Sanderson, David Savill, Kevin Sheehan, Delia Scales and Apollo Stained Glass, Sean Schwegler, Emma Simpson, Christine Stevenson, Mark Stevenson, James Stockman, Tim Sutton, Roger Taylor, Andrew Thearle, Roger Thomas, Mick Viall, Paul Vonberg, Donald Wahlberg, Dave Walsh, Tony Ward, Elaine Warrell, Simon Wartnaby, Ian Whaley, Chris, Susan and Victoria West, Lucy and Vicky Wisada, Alfred Wood, Malcom Woods, Giles Worsley, Sheila Yates, David Yeomans, Gail and Richard Youldon

Blackheath Society,
Greenwich Heritage Centre,
Guildhall Library, Corporation of London,
(the then) Home Office Coroner's Unit,
Lee Manor Society,
Lewisham Local History Archive,
Lewisham Local History Society,
Master and Wardens of the Merchant Taylors' Company,
Master and Wardens of the Plaisterers' Company,
Royal Institute of British Architects Drawings Collection

the residents of the Merchant Taylors' Almshouses, local residents, the community of Lee High Road, passing bus drivers and all our visitors for their interest and encouragement during and after the building work

Selected bibliography

Manuscripts

British Library
Add Mss 5238 Robert Hooke drawings

London Metropolitan Archive
MS01758   Robert Hooke's diary 1672-1688

Merchant Taylor's Company records at the Guildhall Library
*MS34010/10   MTC Court minute books or Records for
              period 1680-90 covering Boone's gift*
MS34010/12   Ditto: for period covering 1720-30
*MS34100/108 Counsel's opinions 1858-1871, complete
              copy of 1683 Indenture and schedule;
              accounts 1724-1824 and various estimates*
MS34100/112 correspondence and 1707 indenture
*MS34101/3   includes partial transcripts of 1683 Indenture
              and Indenture of 1707 signed by Mary
              Boone*
MS34205   Surveyor's report and letter books 1856-83
*MS34214/18   drawings folder including new Boone's
              almshouses up to 1876*
MS34214/19   drawings folder for MTC almshouses, Lee
MS34218   surveyors plan book of estates
*MS34232   Correspondence associated with new CB
              almshouses 1846-1876*

Public Record Office
*Prob/11/385 The Will of Christopher Boone with codicil
              (1686/1686)*
*Prob/11/389 The Will of Christopher Boone with codicil
              (1686/1686)*
Prob/11/584 The Will of Mary Boone (1707/1722)

Royal Institute of British Architects Drawings Collection
*PA183/19(1-3) Plan, south elevation and section of Boone's
              Chapel by Stammers, JR (with Broome, J)
              1935-7; set 3 of 5,
              The other two drawings not in the RIBA
              collection are: north elevation and details
              Boone's Chapel by Broome, J (with
              Stammers, JR) 1935-7, given to Boone's
              Chapel by June Broome through Neil Rhind*

Books

Batten, MI, *The Architecture of Dr. Robert Hooke FRS*,
Walpole Society Jounal 25, London, 1936-7

Bennett, J ed, *London's Leonardo : the life and work of
Robert Hooke*, Oxford, 2003

Beard, G, *The Work of Grinling Gibbons,* London, 1989

Beer, ES de, *The Diary of John Evelyn Vol 3*, Oxford, 1955

Berridge, C, *The Almshouses of London,* Southampton,
1987

Birchenough, J, *Memorials and Inscriptions on Tombstones
in St. Margaret's Lee old church yard,* London, 1967

Birchenough, J, *Some Farms and Fields in Lee*, London,
1980

Brenner, R, *Merchants and Revolution*, London, 2003

Cooper, M, *Robert Hooke and the Rebuilding of London*,
Stroud, 2005

Cowley, R, *The Ancient and Modern Almshouses of South
East London*, 1929, held at Lewisham Local History and
Archives Centre

Davies, M, and Saunders, A, *The History of the Merchant
Taylors' Company*, Leeds, 2004

Drake, HH (ed), *Hasted's History of Kent: Part 1 The
Hundred of Blackheath*, London, 1886

Duncan, LL, *History of the Borough of Lewisham*, London,
1963

Espinasse, M, *Robert Hooke*, London, 1956

Glenister, SH, *Stories of Great Craftsmen*, 1939, reprint
New York City 1977

Gregory, RRC., and Nunn, FW, *The Story of Lee: being records of the ancient parish and parts of its immediate neighbourhood, Parts 1 and 2*, Lewisham, 1923

Hart, FH, *History of Lee and Neighbourhood*, London, 1971

Hasted, E, *The History and Topographical Survey of the County of Kent,* 1797, Kent County Library, Kent 1972.

Howson, B, *Almshouses: a social and architectural history*, Gloucestershire, 2008

Inwood, S, *The Man Who Knew Too Much: the strange and inventive life of Robert Hooke 1635-1703*, London, 2002

Jardine, L, *The Curious Life of Robert Hooke : the man who measured London,* London, 2003

Jardine, L, *On a Grander Scale: the outstanding career of Sir Christopher Wren*, London, 2003

Knoop, D and Jones, GP, *The London Mason of the Seventeenth Century,* Manchester, 1935

Langthorn, JY, *An Archaeological Watching Brief at Boone's Chapel, Lee High Road*, Pre Construct Archaeology Ltd, London, 2006.

Langley, B and T, *The Builders Jewel*, 1741, reprint Abergavenny, 1982

Lysons, D, *The Environs of London Vol 4*, London, 1796

Mills, I, *Craftsmen of St Margaret's*, Knebworth, 2006

Oughton, F, *Grinling Gibbons and The English Woodcarving Tradition*, London 1979

Picard, L, *Restoration London: everyday life in London 1660-1670*, London 2004

Rhind, N, *Blackheath & Environs, Volume I: Blackheath Village & Environs 1790 - 1990: The Village and Blackheath Vale,* Blackheath, 1976

Rhind, N, *Blackheath Village & Environs 1790 - 1990 Volume 2: Wricklemarsh and the Cator Estate, Kidbrooke-Westcombe, The Angerstein Encroachment,* Blackheath, 1983

Robinson, HW, *The Diary of Robert Hooke*, London, 1935

Royal Commission on Historic Monuments, *An Inventory of the Historic Monuments of London, Vol5: East London*, London 1930

Stephenson, C, *Medicine and Magnificence: British hospital and asylum architecture 1660-1815*, New Haven, 2000

Streek, S, *The development of Boone's Estate in Lee, Kent During the C19th*, UCL dissertation, 1998

Summerson, J, *Architecture in Britain 1520-1830*, Hamondsworth, 1977

Strype, J, *Stow's Survey of London*, London, 1720

Target, WD, *The Parish Church of St Margaret*, Lee. London, 1939

Wood, A, *A History of St Margaret's Lee*, London, 1960

Wood, A, *The Christopher Boone's Charity*, London, 1983

Worsley, G, *Taking Hooke Seriously*, Georgian Group Journal 14, 2004

Wren Society, *The Wren Society Volumes, Vols 9, 10, 12, 17, 19, 20*, London 1932-43

Index

© Boone's Chapel Ltd
Published by Boone's Chapel Ltd, Boone's Chapel,
Lee High Road, London SE13 5PH

Further copies of this publication can be obtained from
Boone's Chapel Ltd
www.booneschapel.co.uk, tel: +44 (0)20 8297 4101

ISBN 978-0-9566384-0-3

Stock code _01

Cover image: Tim Crocker Architectural Photography
All images credited to Tim Crocker are ©Tim Crocker.
www.timcrocker.co.uk

Print management by Melanie Jones of MJ Associates
www.em-jays.co.uk

Designed and typeset by Madeleine Adams, Charlie
MacKeith and Rosie Hervey.

Further information about the work of the Blackheath
Historic Buildings Trust can be found at:
www.blackheath.org/bhbt.html

Boone's Chapel

The following pages continuing to the
inside of the rear cover reproduce the
second element of the original charity
legal documentation: the Indenture or
deed.

The Indenture establishes the funding for
the charity as well as the location and
dimensions of its buildings. It also defines
the responsibilities of the Merchant
Taylors' Company on the death of the
founders.

ust Deed Christopher John Boone Esq To The Master And Wardens
The Merchant Tailors Company

is Indenture Tripartite made the two and twentieth day of June in
five and thirtieth yeare of the Reigne of our Sovraigne Lord Charles
second by the Grace of God of England Scotland France and Ireland
g Defender of the Faith P.annoq Dmi 1683 Betweene Christopher
one of London Merchant and Mary his wife of the first part Gilbert
ton of London merchant and Richard Goodall Citizen and
erchant Taylor of London the second parte and the Master and
rdens of the Fraternity of Saint John Baptist in the City of London
the third parte Whereas the said Christopher Boone hath lately
rchased of the Right Honorable Mary Countesse of Feversham the
lief of the Right Honorable George late Earle of Feversham deceased
Honorable Lewis Watson Esq. Sonne and Heir apparent of the
ght Honorable Edward Lord Rockingham and the Lady Katharine
wife only Daughter and Heir of the said Earle of Feversham a
tain parcel of land or wast situate lying and being in the parish of
igh in the County of Kent conteining in breadth fourty foot of assize
it more or less and in length two hundred and tenn foote of assize be
nore or less abutting upon the high way there towards the south upon
comon passage leading over a small Bridge to the parish church of
igh aforesaid towards the west upon a ditch and hedge of a meadow
the said Christopher Boone called brick field towards the north and
on a ditch and pale of another meadow of the said Christopher
one called the two acres towards the east and also one other piece or
rcell of Land or wast in Leigh aforesaid contayning in length ninety
ote of assize be it more or less and in breadth six and twenty foote of
size be it more or less adjoining to the highway aforesaid towards the
uth to a tenement or cottage and yard of William Whitening towards
e west and meadow of the said Christopher Boone now in the
cupation of the said William Whitening towards the north and to a
mon passage leading to the parish church of Leigh aforesaid over a
all bridge towards the east with all and singular the appurtenances
to the said premises or any of them belonging and hath in his
aritable affection and disposition at his owne costs and charges
cted and built upon the said first mentioned piece or parcel of Land
wast severall buildings and edifices hereunder mentioned (that is to
) four Dwellinghouses conteyning each of them one lower roome
arded more than a foote above the ground being sixteene foote of
size and eight inches long or thereabouts and fourteene foote of assize
d eleaven inches broad or thereabouts with a chimney therein and
e upper roome or chamber of the same dimensions in length and
eadth and alsoe one smaller lowe roome or shed with a partition for
er wood coales and the like necessarys fifteene foote of assize long and
ht foote of a size broad or thereabouts on the north side of each said
vellinghouses with a little backyard to each house which said
ildings or Edifices he doth intended for almeshouses and to place
rein one Schoole Mistresse and almspeople intended partly for a
ss platt for dryeing of cloathes a piece or parcell of the said ground
nteyning in length from east to west one hundred fifty and eight foote
assize or thereabouts and in breadth from north to south one and
rty foote of assize or thereabouts at one end whereof is erected and

set up a pump with plenty of water and the other end a convenient
wash house sixteene foote of assize and four inches square or thereabouts
with an oven and some brewing vessels and other utensils therein which
are likewise to be enjoyed and used in common by the said Schoole
Mistresse and almes people together alsoe with two easements or houses
of office the one for the almes men and the other for the almes women
And whereas the said Christopher Boone being minded of his said
charitable dispositions to provide as well for the health of the said
Almes peoples souls as to make provision for the sustenance of their
Bodies hath likewise erected and built upon the said first mentioned
piece or parcell of Land or wast another Building or Edifice at the east
end of the said almes houses containing in length four and twenty foote
of assize and seaven inches or thereabouts and in breadth seaventeene
foote of assize and eight inches or thereabouts and three foote in depth
and six foote in breadth at or under the window on the north and
thereof which east mentioned Edifice or Building he doth intend for a
chappell for the worshipp of Almighty God and hath for that purpose
fitted and furnished the same with a Bell weighing eighty and four
pounds in cubic [?] and with a reading place and Deske and severall
pewes or seates and other accommodacōns and hath made such
provision as hereinafter is likewise expressed for a chaplain to read or
say prayers therein and clarke to attend him in that service & look after
the said Chappell and doth also intend the same for a burying place for
such as he the said Christopher and the said Mary his wife during their
lives and the life of the longer liver of them and after their deceases as
the said Master and Wardens and their successors shall think fit to be
buryed there and doth intend for the purposes aforesaid to procure the
same to be consecrated according to the Rites and Ceremonyes of the
Church of England in such [?] and the said other piece or parcell of
Land or Wast purchased of the said Countesse of Feversham and Lewis
Watson and the Lady Katharine his wife as aforesaid of ninety foote
long and twenty six foote broad is intended and designed by the said
Christopher Boone to be used and enjoyed in common as well by the
said School Mistresse and Almes people as by the proprietors for the
time being in the Capital messuage or Manson House where the said
Christopher now dwellet currently called or known by the name of
Leigh Place for a Dunghill Dungplace or Leystall wherein to cast and
throw their dirt dust and rubbish And whereas the said Christopher
Boone and Mary his wife (being alike charitable minded with him the
said Christopher) doe intend to intend to take upon themselves the
burden of ordering managing and executing their said charitable
intentions and designs for and during the terme of their natural lives
and the life of the longer live of them and afterwards to entreat the said
Master and Wardens and their successors for ever with the governance
management and execution thereof Now the Indenture witnesseth that
the said Christopher Boone for the ends and purposes aforesaid and
for and in consideration of five shillings of lawful money of England to
him in hand paid by the said Gilbert Upton and Richard Goodall at
and before the ensealing and delivery of these presents the receipt
whereof is hereby acknowledged and for divers other good causes and
considerations him thereunto moving hath granted bargained and sold
aliened and confirmed by these presents doth grant bargain and sell
alien and confirm unto the said Gilbert Upton and Richard Goodall

and their heirs all that the said first mentioned piece or parcell of Land or wast conteyning in breath fourty four foote of assize more or less as aforesaid and all and singular the said buildings and edifices and all other the Buildings and edifices Structures and Shedds erected and built or to be erected and built thereon or any parte there of with their and every of their appurtenances (together with free and full liberty of ingresse egresse and regresse way and passage into and out of the said other piece or parcell of Land or wast and the liberty privilege benefit and advantage to cast throw or lay their dung dirt dust ashes and other filth and rubbish into or upon the said last mentioned piece or parcel of Land or wast or any parte thereof and for the making and providing some competent provision for or towards the maintenance of the said Schoole Mistresse and almespeople and for the exercise of divine Service and worshipp in the said Chappell to have continuance for ever and for and in consideration of the further sum of five shillings of like lawful money of England to him the said Christopher in hand paid by the said Gilbert Upton and Richard Goodall at and before the ensealing of these presents the receipt whereof is hereby likewise acknowledged he the said Christopher Boone hath granted bargained and sold aliened and confirmed and by these presents doth grant bargain and sell alien and confirme unto the said Gilbert Upton and Richard Goodall and their heirs all that close peece or parcell of arrable land situate lying and being in the parish of Lee at Leigh near Blackheath in the County of Kent comonly called or known by the name of Berry hill adjoining on the west side to the Lane leading from Lee Town to Lee Church and containing by estimation tenn acres be the same more or less and also all those two closes or parcells of arrable and pasture ground situate in Lee aforesaid near Blackheath in the said County of Kent containing by estimation thirteene acres bee the same more of less adjoining upon the fourth side thereof on the said close called Berry hill and on the north side thereof on the kingshighway leading from Leigh aforesaid to Lewisham which three closes are now and for some time since have been layed into two the one of them still retayning the name of Berryhill but conteyning sixteene acres and an halfe or thereabouts and the same were heretofore containing six acres and an halfe or thereabouts and the same were heretofore in the tenure of Henry Biggs [or] his assigns or undertenants and now are or late were in the tenure of occupation [of] Henry Gryffith or his assigns who holdeth the same of the said Christopher Boone at or under the yearly rente of fifteene pounds and all ways passages profits comodities and advantages to the said severall closes and parcels of Land and premises with the appurtenances belonging on in any wise appertaining or therewith on with any of them used occupied or enjoyed as part parcell or member And alsoe all that annual rent or Fee Farme Rent of two and fourty poundes of lawfull money of England reserved and issuing out of and for the Fee Farme if the City of Hereford now or late paid or payable by the Citizens of the said City of Hereford which said Fee Farme Rent by one Indenture Tripartite enrolled in the His Majesties Court of Chancery bearing date the sixteenth day of September one thousand six hundred and seaventy and two made or mentioned it be made betweene the Right Honorable Francis Lord Hawley Sir Charles Harbord Sir William Hawood and Sir John Talbot Knights and William Harbord Esquire Trustees for the sale of the Fee Farme Rents and other rents

(Sir Robert Stewart Knight another Trustee for the Sale if the same Rents being then dead) of the first parte Sir John Bancks Barronett of the second parte and Joseph Hornby Citizen and Goldsmith of London and Nathaniell Hornby and John Orton Citizens and Haberdashers of London of the third parte was for the consideracōns therein mentioned granted and conveyed to the said Jasper Hornby Nathaniell Hornby and John Orton and their heirs and by one other indenture bearing date the tenth day of march one thousand six hundred seaventy and two likewise enrolled in His Majesties said Court of Chancery and made or mentioned to be made betweene the said Joseph Hornby Nathaniell Hornby and John Orton of the first parte and the said Christopher Boone of the other parte was for the considerations therein mentioned granted and conveyed to the said Christopher Boone and his Heirs and the revertion and revertions remainder and remainders rents issues and profits of all and singular the premises hereby granted or mentioned to be granted and every part and parcell thereof and all the estate right title interest clayme and demand whatsoever of him the said Christopher Boone of in and to the same every or any part thereof Together with all Deeds Evidences and writings touching or concerning the premises only or any part or parcell thereof onely which hee the said Christopher Boone hath in his custody or can come by without suit in Law and true copyes of all such deeds and writings in the custody of the said Christopher which he can come by as aforesaid as concerne the premises or any part thereof togeather with any other Lands tenements or hereditaments To have and to hold the said two pieces or parcells of Land or wast and all and singular the said Buildings Edifices and Structures erected and built or to be erected and built thereon the said pieces of Land and closes of arrable and pasture in Lee aforesaid and the said annual rent or Fee Farme rent of two and fourty pounds and all and singular other the premises with their and every of their appurtenances herein before granted or mentioned to be granted unto the said Gilbert Upton and Richard Goodall and their Heirs for ever to the uses intents and purposes and the ends and upon and under the trusts hereinafter limited declared and expressed that is to say To the use and behoofe of the said Christopher Boone and Mary his wife for and during the tenure of their naturall lives and the life of the longer liver of them and from and after the decease of the said Christopher and Mary and the longer liver of them to the use and behoofe of the said Master and Wardens of the Merchant Tailors of the Fraternity of St. John Baptist in the City of London and their successors for ever Upon trust and confidence neverthelesse and to the end and intent that they said Master Wardens of the said Company and their successors shall from and after the said premises shall come into their possession by virtue of these presents out of the rents issues and profits thereof allow and duly pay or cause to be paid unto the Chaplains of the said Chappell for the time being for his paynes taken in the Service of the said Chappell the annuall sume of tenn pounds and unto the Clarke of the said Chappell the annual sume of two pounds and unto the said Schoole Mistresse seaven pounds per annum at the two most usual feasts or days of payment in the yeare by even and equall process that is to say the Feast of the annunciation of the blessed Virgin Mary and Feast of Saint Michael the Archangel the first payment thereof to begin and be made at such of the said Feasts as shall first happen after the decease of the said Christopher Boone and Mary his wife and th longer liver of them and upon this further trust and confidence th they the said Master Wardens of the said Company shall out of th rents issues and profits of the premises after the same shall come in their possession as aforesaid allow and pay unto the said Schoo Mistresse for the time being yearly and every year at the Feast of Sai Michael the Archangel the sume of two poundes over and above th said yearly sume of seaven poundes before appointed to be paid un her for wood or coales and shall also pay or cause to be paid to the s poor almes people twelve pence a piece every week to buy them brea making such recompense and satisfaction to such person or perso where they shall think fit to employ or intrust to pay the same as th shall think fit to employ or intrust to pay the same as they shall think for his or their trouble in paying the same by weekly payments and ter shillings per annum to find firing [?] and twenty shillings a piece eve Feast of the birth of our Lord God and upon this further trust that th said Master Wardens of the said Company and the successors shall o of the rents issues and profits of the premises after the same shall con into their possession from time to time as there shall be occasion provic a common prayer Book for the use of the said Chappell Bibles ar Testaments for the use of the said poor almes people psalters gown and horn books and also needles scissors knitting needles thread si samples and the like necessaries for the use of the said poor children be taught by the said Schoole Mistresse as aforesaid which as the sa Christopher Boone does compute will not amount to above four shillings per annum inasmuch as he doth intend to leave the sa Chappell and almes houses well furnished with those provisions at th time as the said company of their successors shall come to have th charge thereof and upon this further trust that they the said Mast Wardens of the said Company and their successors after the sa premises into their possession aforesaid shall lay up and preserve th residue or overplus of the rents issues and profits of the premises whic as the said Christopher Boone doth compute will amount to eleave poundes thirteene shillings per annum or thereabouts to be a Stock Bank to defraye the charge of repairs and other casualties and incide charges in and about the premises and the management and executio thereof and upon this further trust that they the said Master Warder of the said Company and their successors after the said premises sho come into their possession as aforesaid shall take upon them the charg and governance of the said Chappell and almes houses and of th governing ordering and directing choosing placing and displacing th said Chaplaine Clerke Schoole Mistresse almes people and poo children and of managing and executing the whole charitable desig aforesaid and things thereunto belonging according to the Rules Orde and Ordinances conteyned in a Schedule indented hereunto annexe and such further or other lawfull and reasonable rules orders ar ordinances as the said Christopher Boone at any time during the term of his natural life or the said Mary Boone if she shall survive him durin the terme of her natural life shall by any writing under their respecti handes make ordaine & constitute with the consent and approbatio of the said Master Wardens of the said Company their successors assignes and for that end that the said Master Wardens Company an their successors shall once every yeare on the first Thursday of Ju